SOUTH CE

CRIPS

The story of the South Central L.A. street gang
from 1971-1985

DONALD BAKEER

To Astan,
Congratulations
on a great choice.
Inshallah you will
be granted Allah's peace.
As Salaamu Alaikum
[signature]
5/13/2K

Precocious Publishing/Los Angeles

Precocious Publishing Co.
P.O. Box 2619, Inglewood, CA 90305-0619
Fourth Precocious Printing

ISBN 0-9634969-0-5

Special Thanks For
assisting in the research
and addition of anecdotes:

Laurence (L.C. Shabazz) Fortenbury
Aadil Naazir
Sherry Coppage
John Abdul Hasan
Charles El Amin
Muhammad Abdullah
Sheikh Tajuddin B. Shu'aib
Sharon Bakeer
Aswan (Doc) Spry (R.I.P.)
The Hoover Crip Gang (HCG)
The Eight Tray Gangsters (ETG)
The Rolling Sixty Crips (RSC)
Tee Rodgers
The Blood Nation
The Griot Spirits
Edna Crutchfield &
The International Black Writers and Artists
Muhammad Ali
All the Los Angeles area Muslims
Father Aamde and The Watts Prophets
Hilton Jordan
Maulana Karenga
L.A.U.S.D.

CRIPS

CHAPTER I

Mr. Crenhaw's Wall Must Fall

If he just had the nerve. He needed guts, and it was any day, now, before he was sure he was going to feel some growing deep in the pit of his stomach near his bowels, and they were going to take a reverse path. Then he would have them -- guts! Then he would write on that big, pretty, pink wall there, too. He would show Old Mean Mr. Crenshaw that he had gone too far with the wrong boy, this time.

'That's a very bad boy for 8 years old', thought Willie Crenshaw. The youngster was a con artist, and just natural bad luck and news. But, he still should not have shot the kid. Even he had to admit that the kid had made him lose his head.

Yeah, "The Kid", "The Li'l Baby", his B.K.A.(Better Known As). Li'l Jimmie could just imagine it... laying there for everybody to see. 'Mr. Crenshaw's wall must fall.'

It was beautiful, a pretty, pink, block wall that (he was ashamed to say) he could barely see over. And, on the other side of which he could see the house that he could never go into and children that he could never play with.

Willie Crenshaw was born on the West Side of Los Angeles, the product of a century of yearning. He had meant to move on 109th and Main Street for a quick real estate investment, then get out. But, the world was closing in on him. He had been here for nine years and a lot of people were saying property had peaked. Interest rates had reached 18% on first mortgages and his real estate investment was being frozen right up under him. Sex was always on his mind, and now he had this eight year old kid turning his own wife against him. You would think your own wife would back you just on the strength of being your wife, but see that's what you get when you marry somebody out of Dorsey High. You just could not trust a bourgeois broad.

"So what if the kid's momma is in trouble cause her man has gone to the majestic palatial county jail for a sojourn. The dude has been gone an awful long time. The dude was a sap, anyway." Willie held out his hand for an obligatory five. After all he was buying the beer.

"Sure you right," co-signed his drinking partner, Popeye, still not sure which kid he was talking about.

"And the momma is doing the... the unthinkable," Willie giggled drunkenly.

"Sure you right, and you know you right," chorused Popeye.

"They can all die," Willie was on a roll.

"Naw, man, you don't understand. They are not your enemies," said Brother Less, breaking the spell.

"They are our friends, huh?" said Willie, his mind going back to the grinning face of little Jimmie Willie Black at his bedroom window. By the time he had stopped laughing at the irony of the intimate escapade that the little burglar must have seen... "Burglar!" 'What was the kid doing in his yard?'

Crazy Willie (his high school moniker) had felt a gripping sensation in his gut. The unmistakable urge gnawed at his entrails. It was more gripping than sexual lust. It was a ripened lust to kill a human being.

He reached for his shotgun by the bed and ran out of the screen door into the August night, pausing only momentarily to put on his robe. His mind moved into second gear.

'What happens if I kill a burglar? How did I know it was a kid? Better get close so I don't accidentally shoot up somebody's house.'

A small form scaled the wall with one beautiful feline leap. His silhouette against the crimson night sky flexed against the penetration of the pellets. As if to say 96 months of life is not enough for this awful experience, but the skin relented and Jimmie was immediately flung into Main Street.

His mind went back to the moment before his decision to leap -- the sound of the big street in the distance. All the cars and people were protection. If he could just make it to Imperial, Mr. Crenshaw couldn't kill him. He had left the weighty water hose underneath the car. He was hurt but he wouldn't let the bullet kill him. It was fire in his back, and he fought to keep his consciousness, but somehow the voice that was meant to scare him was too far away. The only thing real was the pain in his back.

"Don't kill him," Brother Less had shouted with just enough emotion to jolt Willie back into first gear.

'A Witness!'

"He was in my yard.., stealing. Let me kill him," Willie pleaded, now, fearful but not yet ashamed.

"He ain't your enemy, but I can't stop you," Brother Less could see the all too familiar, yet, special hatred in Willie Crenshaw's contorted frame. Yeh, Crazy Willie wanted that first kill, badly. His muscles tensed and his voice was straining, almost hysterical.

"The lawyers and bail bondsmen will bleed you dry, Willie." Brother Less's reasoning climbed in between the anger and the act. Again, the street reasoning had prevailed.

The liquor store drinking buddies were about equally divided on the issue, and the emotion was high. But, the men in their mid-30's who climbed out of their worries and into their bottles (Bro. Less only drank so-da) at this very unspecial spot each day were mostly veterans of high school street riots. They had all been members of the US Organization or the Black Panthers or Black Muslims in the tumultuous 1960's at Fremont, Jordan or Locke High School, and though the flames of revolution had smouldered, this particular peer group could not help but consider and reconsider when confronted with the actuality of taking another soul brother's life.

Somehow, they felt what they decided mattered more than the latest policy of 77th Street Division of the Police Department. Even in 1978 men were still the strongest force in the South Central L. A. community, and they were some of the strongest men.

The young brothers in some neighborhoods were rude to the police and ruthless to any show of weakness, but they tripped around Big Brother Less and Watt's finest with the utmost respect. Why kill one because he was full of juice?

Finally, there was accord, begrudging ascension to the code of unanimity for Willie, but it had cost him $400 to make bail though he was never arraigned because of the "public outcry at the thought of one of their upstanding young father's being charged with a crime for reacting courageously in defense of his family."

A lot of people in the neighborhood looked at Willie with a strange respect now. He was about to convince himself that he was the hero that the papers made him out to be. The women loved that kind of stuff, and Willie loved the women.

Except for the once and a while pain in his back that reminded Jimmy that he had still better take it a little cool, getting shot was the greatest thing he had ever done. Everybody had come to visit him at Martin Luther King Hospital, and he had stayed there a whole month. Clean sheets and all he could eat. The hospital was spank brand new and the smells were enough to make you want to live. He loved the alcohol smell. It meant clean and the nurses patted him and kissed him goodnite.

After he graduated from his wheel chair (chauffeur driven) to shuffling around in the pink house shoes that Nurse Shelley had bought him, he had been introduced to what was now his favorite game, Ping Pong. It fascinated him. He monopolized the table. Floundering at first, but before long he was beating all but the best players. Nurse Shelley had shown him how to play, but he beat her regularly before long. It seemed strange that the more he beat her, the more she made over him.

"Be careful, Jimmie, it's time to lay down."

It was like he was her only patient. He knew she felt sorry for him, but there was something else. He felt it when she hugged him tight after he said he wished she were his mother, his face pushed comfortably against her firm bosom. He held on tight, his mind racing. He needed a woman in his life, and he hoped he didn't ever have to let her go.

He shouldn't have made that doctor dude look so bad on the ping pong table or who knows, he could still be waking up on that hill in Watts, looking out the window at the Watts Towers, comfortable and safe.

But, now, he was home, and his mother was taking out her hatred for his father on him.

"You no good. You just a no good yellow dog like your Daddy..."

It no longer hurt. It just mounted up and up and began to sag like a heavy load. Yeh, sure, he knew he was her biggest problem, the family's biggest problem, the world's biggest problem, as she often called him, but what could he do about it? He was only eight, and if he was just like his daddy, it was his daddy's fault. He should have hated his father, too, but he really didn't remember him that well.

Things got so bad that he was either put out of the house or running away so much that he very seldom saw his mother. When they happened to cross each other's path in the small apartment, she just grunted at him and frowned. She never cooked for him or gave him any money. She got up each morning, went to work and assumed he went to school. On weekends he seldom stayed at home. If his mother wanted to tell him something, she would tell his older sister, Tanya, who also hated him. But, Jimmie could handle Tanya. He was blackmailing her.

Tanya was the spitting image of her midnight dark, tight' pantsed gluteus maximus mother. They both shared a shameless penchant for light skinned curly haired pimpish men. It was strange that they didn't like Jimmie who was the spitting image of his dad.

Tanya was determined to get pregnant by somebody that, hopefully, nobody around the neighborhood knew, and she would go bus riding often and return with some light skinned Lothario with his pants bulging. They always eventually ended up arguing. Usually because the men began to flaunt their other women. It was amazing that they all knew her weakness. The worse they treated her, the more she loved them. Fortunately, none of them were immune to the criminal environment so they soon wound up in jail. Neither were they very virile because Tanya still waited for her first baby to be born.

Jimmie the Kid had taken the opportunity to snap a picture of his sister at a most frenetically perverse moment with one of her lovers. The Polaroid camera had been his most prized possession before his mother found most of his secret pictures (various family members and friends on the toilet, dogs eating doo doo, etc.). The kind of stuff that had put him in the third grade hall of fame with his male peers had sent her into a violent, screaming, frenzy before making a wildeyed ceremony of the burning.

Only the picture of his sister and her lover with his eyes bulging had remained. This he used to force Tanya into doing what he needed, and he needed her help even more since he had been shot.

His mother seemed to think his overwhelming blame in the incident had canceled out the need for compassion, and Jimmie couldn't bear to show her that he needed her. So, he threatened Tanya with the graphic description of his hidden picture and she did, begrudgingly, for him what most sisters would have done out of compassion. She fixed him food, and changed his bandage (but she insisted on screeching and squealing at the sight of his ugly wound). She did what he needed her to do for him, but it had nothing to do with her sense of love or responsibility for him. In fact, no longer did his mother feel responsible for him either.

No need. He was almost well, now, and he didn't really need either of them.

Willie Crenshaw leered at Jimmie as the boy walked past. You would not think that the kid would have the audacity to even walk on the same side of the street, but there he was ambling by. And, what was he looking at so intently? Or what was he looking for? He was sure that kid was looking at something on his brick wall. Well, I'll be damned. You'd think that he would have the sense to be afraid, but he acts as if he has forgotten that I had him at death's door only 3 months ago. Willie's heartbeat quickened as he saw his coffee colored wife rush out to the gate with a napkin full of cookies for the kid. She felt like she owed him. She would explain if he dared ask her again. It was a very touchy subject with her. She felt, somehow, as if she had been responsible for this poor little boy being given even another woe.

Was that why she wouldn't come to him anymore? Didn't it all start about the same time? "I could kill him," he heard his mouth ejaculate.

Chapter 2

The Shooting

The tall, slender framed man moved with a military precision. Jimmie watched from under the bushes as he got out of the cab. The man seemed to do everything fast. The cabbie's smile beamed after shaking his passenger's hand. It was as if he had chauffeured a dignitary of the highest magnitude. Jimmie had never seen two men treat each other so kindly.

"As Salaamu Alaikum," said the thin man.

"Wa Alaikum As Salaam," came the cabbie's reply.

The tall passenger walked right by Jimmie's bush, sunlight reflecting off his black shiny shoes. He didn't knock on the door, but burst in. It was only then that Jimmie recognized his daddy from the back. The back of his head protruded and almost hooked under. It had been a long time and Big Jimmie had changed, but though he was smaller than the man he remembered, this fine black man was his daddy. Suddenly, Jimmie wanted to have him hold him. He felt very young and strange. It was like he wanted to cry, but couldn't.

Big Jimmie grabbed his wife's behind with both hands. She flinched, but only for the slightest instant. Her Jimmie was home! Her blood sang. She whirled and the tears flew out of her eyes. She kissed him a long soap opera kind of kiss. He caressed her. It was a long time before they talked.

"Why didn't you tell me you were getting out, Baby. I shoulda gotten my hair done."

"It don't matter, Baby, cause I'm back now and it's all right. It's all going to be all right, now."

"I cursed you, Jimmie. I hated you for going to jail and leaving us. I didn't know how to do nothing. I hadn't never worked. People gonna tell you everything about me," Carole cried softly, confessionally.

"Don't worry, sweet black baby, I'm back, now, and things have changed. All praises due to Almighty God Allah."

For weeks the bedroom door in the little one bedroom apartment was closed and latched almost all of the time when Big Jimmie was at home. When it was opened, and he stepped out almost majestically, Big Jimmie cracked orders and jokes in a new voice that bore no similarity to the voice that Jimmie Jr. only faintly recollected. This new voice was beautiful to hear. It had an electricity and confidence in it. Not that Big Jimmie was often home. He was a frenzy of movement. He had whipped Jimmie Jr. senseless, but somehow there was a feeling so strong and wonderful between them that it made them both smile just to look at each other.

Of course Jimmie Jr. was grown by the time his father returned from prison. He had done all the things that it took to be a man. Most of them were sexual and girls were always ready, willing and capable since he had stopped attending school and had started running with the 107 Hoover Crips, the local gang. There were almost as many kids on the streets during school hours as there were at Woodcrest Elementary. After Jimmie had gotten out of the hospital, he had not gone back to school because of his stitches. The habit stuck even after the stitches had come out.

He still got up every morning just as though he were going to third grade, but he would head straight to the vacant lot on 116th and Figueroa. The city was in the slow process of clearing land for a freeway and his "Wanna Be Hoover Crip" friends could go from Avalon to Vermont on 116th Street and there was nothing but vacant land. In fact, the strip went all the way through Inglewood on the West and past Watts on the East, but that was very unfriendly territory, especially Watts where Grape Street Crips and Bounty Hunters (Bloods) were on every corner, or so it seemed.

Jimmie's regular routine was to go to the vacant lot

every morning, kick it with his homeboys until they got tired, maybe do a little slap boxing, talk about who had gotten shot or killed lately, and who had gotten out of or put into jail.

"Bear just got out of the county, Cuzz. You know that fool gonna kill some people. Somebody got to die, Cuzz. He 74 Hoover O.G. (Original Gangster). Anybody crossed his name off the wall while he was locked down is gonna die," said Termite, Jimmie's main homeboy. Termite knew all the news on the gangster set. He was down with all of the O.G. 107's. Termite bragged that he was born a Crip.

"My daddy was a member of the original 107 Hoover Crip Gang, the original Crips in Los Angeles, O.G. to the max. When he got killed my momma tied a little blue handkerchief around my neck and took me to the funeral, Cuzz. I still remember and I was only 4. I'm twelve, now. That's over 8 years ago." Termite loved telling the story of how a rival gang had pulled out guns at the funeral and shot his father's body again in the casket.

"Bool ya Bool ya! There was a big shootout at the funeral, Cuzz. That's why they have so many security at Crip funerals, now. And, don't never go to a funeral without wearing your blue rag so everybody can see, Cuzz. Show the world. Crips Don't Die. They Multiply."

Jimmie would tell the story of how he had gotten shot and lie about the details which he felt a little guilty about but couldn't help. He was the youngest in their set, but he was the only one who had ever really been shot (several Wanna Be's claimed to have been shot at) so he was accepted and admired. Sometimes he would show them the still partially unhealed wound amidst a chorus of"ooh's" and "wow's".

Termite, D-Bone, Li'l Mad Dog, Boody and about ten other homeboys held down the set in the lot on Fig. Most of the homeboys went to school most days and cut out once in a while to be with their homies in the lot, but Termite, D-Bone, Li'l Mad Dog, Boody and lately Jimmie The Kid (his Crip name) only went up to the school after it was over to rob the boys and terrorize the girls.

They hung around the school yard playing basketball until everybody left and hit up the walls with their names in spray paint. Jimmie had learned to use the spray can much quicker and much better than he did a pencil or pen. He had always hated to print his name on his papers at school. He was always ashamed of his work and his signature was sometimes laughed at by the little cute girls who wrote like the pen was a part of their finger. But, give him a spray can and he could write *ThE KiD* and *107 HCG* like Crips twice his age.

That's why everybody knew he was going to be O.G as soon as he was old enough. As soon as he got some guts, he was going to hit up every wall in his neighborhood, especially old mean Mr. Crenshaw who had tried to kill him. He dreamed of walking past his B. K. A. on Mr. Crenshaw's pretty, pink, block wall fence and looking him straight in the eye and saying, "Yeh, I'm a Crip you fool."

That would take guts to tell everybody he was a Crip. Jimmie and Termite had been entertaining the homeboys with their stories and somebody had come up with some grass. It had seemed so natural and peaceful just laying in the grass smoking grass that they didn't notice the 2 black and whites converge on them. The four police were on them before they knew it.

"Don't move, you nappyhead bastards."

The words were still being formed in his mouth when Jimmie and Termite had left them in the distance. They leaped like young deer in the tall grass. They zigged and zagged then on cue split in two directions. They knew the cops wouldn't shoot them in the daytime, and they sure couldn't catch them. Their slower reacting friends were being handcuffed and poked with clubs by three of the policemen, and the other cop was dead on Jimmie's tail.

Jimmie jumped the wall that separated the lot and the Figueroa sidewalk and dove head first underneath a parked car just before the cop's hand could grab his shaggy hair. He slid on his belly and pushed with his knees until he came out on the street side of the car. He ran straight across the street without looking or caring. The cop stopped for the traffic and screamed at the two men standing in front of the Imperial Liquor store and Deli Market.

"Stop that kid. Hold him!"

The scraggly faces of the men turned slowly towards the commotion. They saw the disheveled, frustrated cop, at the same moment the frantically fleeing youngster ran between them.

"Should we have grabbed him?" said one.

"Can a blind hog see his butt?" answered his drinking buddy.

"Burn rubber. Burn, baby, burn. Run, run, fly, don't stop. Just make it to Avalon."

When Jimmie got to Avalon, one block north of Imperial, he turned into a backyard and flopped on the ground straining for his breath. His face and stomach throbbed with cuts, and his back hurt too. All of a sudden his back hurt him worst of all. Had the policeman shot him, after all?

The thought of being shot again made the pain unbearable, Yeh, he was shot and in the same place. He touched his back and the now familiar dark red blood was spurting out. All he could do was go home. If he didn't he would die. His momma would take him to the hospital after she hollered her lungs out at him... No, his daddy would take him. His daddy would understand. He could tell his daddy almost anything. Maybe even that he was a Crip. Even that he had quit school. His daddy would understand. His daddy wouldn't let him die.

When Jimmie Jr. collapsed thru the screen door onto the living room floor, his mother and sister did not react right away. It was too unbelievable, too horrible to deal with. The ambivalence of their relationship to this wretched, little pile of bones and skin bleeding all over the carpet froze them in front of the television.

Big Jimmie had seen his son tottering up the steps and into the house from his car as he pulled up. He didn't bother to park. He turned off the ignition and leaped out. The splotches of blood on the sidewalk were too big. There wasn't much blood in an eight year old. He barked orders as he bent over his son.

"Tanya, bring me a towel, towels and cold water! Carole call the paramedics, and tell them to make it fast... Call the operator if you don't know the number, and stop that crying. That ain't helping nothing."

When Big Jimmie had finally cleaned the wound, he saw a big hole, the size of a fist in the boy's side and back.

"I'm shot, Daddy," little Jimmie barely whispered. His daddy pressed the wet towels down on it, but the blood would not stop completely. 'Where was the damn ambulance?'

He looked out the window and saw a flashing red light. Funny, he hadn't heard their siren, but at least they were here. Maybe Little Jimmie would make it.

"Go tell them to hurry," he said to Tanya just before the policemen came in haughtily.

"Is this your son, sir?"

The disappointment and weariness shone as he said meekly,
"Yes, I..."

"I'm afraid he's under arrest. He resisted arrest and fled earlier, and my partner and I..."

"You shot him. You shot him cause he ran-- an eight year old kid. You devils!" The dam broke in Big Jimmie, he kept the towel pressed firmly on his son's wound but he cursed and threatened the police.

By this time a crowd had gathered in front of the first floor apartment on Main Street. The rumor of little Jimmie being shot by the police was on everybody's lips.

The policeman who had chased little Jimmie instinctively put his hand on his revolver. He turned to his partner in amazement.

'Blanton had not made mention of having shot the kid, but he may have done it. Why? How could he hate these kids so much? These were the times that tried men's souls,' thought Officer Johnnie Johnson as he looked just to the southeast at Locke High School where he had graduated 5 years ago.

The crowd grew sullen and more ominous.

"Break it up. This is police business," Ofc. Blanton droned, not wanting to sound too emotional but officious and insistent. The sea of angry faces stood between the two officers and their patrol car. It was obvious that it would take force to get through them and call for help. The father continued to curse them, and the little boy lay dying on the carpeted floor. The crowd didn't move, didn't seem to breathe. No longer did it seem a crowd of people to the policeman but a black mass of hatred.

"Go on back home," came the faceless but familiar voice. "You can't help, so go on home. You'll just be in the way when the ambulance comes. Don't keep the boy from getting help!"

It was Brother Less cajoling and careful as a lion tamer. He let them leave with dignity and pride. The ambulance soon came and the paramedics removed Big Jimmie's hand from his son's side. He leaped in the back of the ambulance and shot murderous glances at the two cops as Ofc. Blanton spieled his much practiced speech and silently said his Hail Mary's without crossing his chest.

Chapter 3
In the Beginning

Jimmie Black Sr. was hardly the kind of black man that you would think would become a Muslim, but he was jailed and humiliated when he was on top of the street game at 22. Jail had been hanging over his head for two years before he finally went, but he hadn't expected it. It cut him to his viscera.

He had lost his spirit by the time they finally locked him down. He tried to think, but all he could see was the judge's expressionless face saying, "I sentence you to the state penitentiary for a term of not more than 10 nor less than 3 years."

Carole screamed and fought with the bailiffs to try to get to him. He could still hear her screaming and fighting as the elevator door closed and they took him from the County Courts Building to the County Jail to await his transfer to Tehachapi.

He didn't want to talk to any of the other prisoners. It was a mistake. The second night in the County Jail he had been attacked by a gang of five prisoners who tried to turn his rivers around.

When he arrived at Tehachapi, he was terrified. But, Islam came to him, and he fled to embrace it. It was immediately his salvation. It was the missing piece in his, heretofore, puzzling, make-it-up-as-you-go-along philosophy.

Jimmie reflected on a history of growing up light and cute with curly, New Orleans style hair in Watts. Markham Junior High School and Jordan, then Locke High. He didn't fit. Women kept him in trouble wherever he went. They flocked to him, but the gold was cursed. He had given up being cute and quit school and started being tough.

He probably would have made it pretty well, too, as a small time hustler and part time player, but he met Carole, his first and only love. She had a daughter, and he was in love in high school. It didn't matter that she was 3 years older than him and had a 6 year old daughter.

Carole was padded everywhere that it counted, and yellow and black made pretty babies. They started staying together on 116th and Figueroa while he was still in high school at Locke.

Carole was on the county and it was sweet. She was a steamy black brickhouse, who just loved to bring Jimmie money. He had "no idea where she was getting the money," but the police said he was pandering. Jimmie reflected on how, ironically, she had gotten him his first criminal record. After he got out of jail, he had a pimp's reputation, and he decided that he might as well try the life of crime because he already had a record, and probably couldn't get a job.

When he went back to Carole, she was doing bad. She was strung out on the new drug, P-C-P. It was a rollercoaster.

He would have to beat her up badly to bring her to her senses. She couldn't even stay on the county. She sent little Tanya to live with the child's grandmother. Carole looked bad, real bad, but Jimmie was in love and he vowed to see her through it.

Things were really bad when Carole got pregnant. She didn't know herself for 3 months because she was taking birth control pills, diet pills and vitamins and who knows what else.

"Jimmie, I ain't got no damn money, and I need some pills."

"How much? How many?"

"5 or 6 dollars. I need some birth control pills. You don't want no little Jimmie Jr. sucking on these breasts. You freak you." It cut him the way she disdained him, nowadays.

"Might not be so bad, if he looked like me, cause you know what Ray Charles says."

"What?"

"If you have 100 babies, girl, just so they all look like me."

"That ain't it."

And they argued, and they argued. They couldn't stay in the tiny kitchenette with the couch that let out into the bed without arguing. Jimmie was losing his best friends because of his "big butt problem."

"I'm putting you down, square. You can't even control your woman. Down her, man, or better, yet, give her to me. I'll put her in line. You'll be better off Li'l J.".

"I must admit I am looking to drop her next time I strike gold. Let's go hustle out at Hollywood Park. Have you noticed there's a lot of beating up going down on the streets? Li'l Chino said he just walked over on Figueroa last night and got jumped by everybody," said Jimmie who was always wary of the beat up because he was light in the face and in the behind, and some people, mistakenly, thought he was a mark.

"They gonna lose, Cuzz. We got too many homeboys on Hoover. Too many killers on Hoover. You know it yourself, Cuzz," replied Fass Black, a.k.a. Ray Ray, Ray Dog, and a number of other nicknames that went on ad infinitum.

"We are the baddest thing on the streets. Let's go show it. We'll strut in cool -- walking cool -- and take over Figueroa. The streets haven't seen this much force since Watts in '65. Then we'll strut out."

The Century bus seemed especially slow. They could hardly run down their 3 card monte game in the race track parking lot for thinking about their big plans for that night.

Jimmie told Carole, and she wanted to come. They argued, but she came anyway. Jimmie remembered how comfortable the leather shoulder holster and .357 magnum felt. He was 17 and mean, and he had yearned to take an aimed shot at a human being.

Sure enough the word swept like riot fever, and by 7:30 P.M. there were so many bouncing low riders, V.W.'s, and strollers on 107th and Hoover that Fass Black decided to leave early. He told everybody to turn their radios off and walk quiet and cool as they turned the corner of 109th and Fig. The air stood still. They blocked the whole intersection.

Suddenly, a car pulled down Figueroa going north and stopped. It was Jay Stone in the car with a trick driving, but instead of going into the motel on the east side of the street, the trick walked into an apartment on the west side of Figueroa near the middle of the block.

All of a sudden they heard Jay Stone's woman scream. The trick was beating her up. All the Figueroa prostitutes, players, and pimps looked at Jay standing by the trick's Cadillac. He tried to play nonchalant, but he eyed the gangsters blocking the street and knew this was a hot moment.

The trick came out, his blonde hair mussed, but he was smiling. Fass Black broke for him. He was tough, but Black was kicking him, now. All of a sudden he went for his pocket and about 3 people shot him at the same time. Jimmie was one of the shooters. They strutted back over to 107th and Hoover.

When they asked Fass Black what he called their cripple walk, he said it was cooler than cripple. It was the Crip walk or CArip walk.

The next edition of the Los Angeles Sentinel published a dramatic description of the scenario and called the gang from 107th and Hoover the Crips.

Chapter 4
The Baby

Carole had the baby at Cedar's Sinai Hospital in Beverly Hills on her Medi Cal card. The baby boy slowed her down a little bit. She actually nursed the baby. Everybody was so surprised, but her doctor, Dr. Brown, who just happened to be light skinned and handsome, talked her into it. He, also talked her out of poisoning her body with drugs just before the baby came.

Everybody said that the baby turned her around. She was so proud of little Jimmie Willie Black Jr. that she pushed her little baby carriage up and down Figueroa from Imperial to their apartment complex on 116th all day long.

They eventually had to move because Figueroa had become exclusively for whores, day and night. Carole's 7 year old daughter was staying with them, again, and Jimmie was sure that she was about to be turned out.

They moved to some real fancy apartments on the West Side, in what was appropriately called L.A.'s Jungle. The area at the foot of Baldwin Hills was landscaped with palm trees and shrubbery everywhere you looked. The rent was high, $200, but there was a pool, and Jimmie wanted Jimmie Jr. to grow up on the West Side of Los Angeles. He didn't know, really, how far away it was.

The Jungle was full of people from out of town and in this apartment were some con artists and hit men from Kansas City. Jimmie was really good with cards, craps and women, so they had a lot in common.

Before long, Gene, the self appointed and viciously empowered leader of the Kansas City crew, and Jimmie opened an after hours gambling joint on the Crenshaw strip. It was a real den of iniquity, meant to service every illicit urge. The money was coming fast for everybody.

Jimmie parked his rented Benz in the stall behind the apartment, pulled down his straw and strolled past the swimming pool in his apartment building. Carole hollered at him from the other side of the pool where she lay sunning her ample, smooth, honey-black body, her bosom heaving from a finished swim --heaving and fairly bursting her bathing suit. Every man's eye in the building was on her. It was this way whenever she went swimming.

Jimmie turned and went over to pick up his son when Genie Lamp called him from the apartment at the top of the stairs.

"What's happening, Slick Jimmie? Come on up and toot one, get your splivvins together."

Jimmie wasn't really into tooting, but he did want to talk to Genie Lamp. It seemed he had lived on the lip of peril. He had almost died a thousand deaths in Kansas City, but what Jimmie most admired was, Lamp was a killer, and men sharpened men. The only thing he didn't like about him was that he seemed to have an insatiable appetite for drugs of all kinds, even heroin and cocaine. He drank. He smoked. He ate everything, and he devoured women. It seemed Lamp wanted to partake of everything life had to offer before he went back to prison, and he was sure to go back.

"I got some doojie, man. I thought you might wanna toot it," said Lamp sifting the pile of white powder with a small gold spoon. "This is good stuff. Come on. Get like me – TOASTED!!"

Jimmie took a short straw and imitated Lamp. He was sure that he couldn't get strung out tooting, but he had never done the Big Bad Boy before. Seemed like all the heavy hustlers were either tooting or shooting and most were doing both.

It seemed like the heroin went straight to his brain. He dropped off in a heavy nod. Half sleep, half awake, all mellow. His arms were heavy and it seemed like Lamp was talking super fast, but his movements were very slow. Jimmie lay back on the long furry, white couch at a 45 degree angle. He began to survey the room. The low mirrored coffee table was luxurious and strewn with cigarettes and jewelry. There were 3 butts in the ashtray -- two with lipstick on them. The pack lay next to the ashtray, Kool100's just like Carole smoked. His sense of smell heightened, and the incense made him sneeze. It almost covered up the sickening, sweet smell of P-C-P.

He let his body go limp and rocked forward with the force of 1,2,3,4 successive sneezes. When his nose finally returned control of his body to him, he had moved two feet down on the couch. His hands came to rest in the soft furry couch. His left hand felt something silky. He raised his hand with the silky, white, slightly wet drawers. Something about them almost aroused him. He glanced across the coffee table and saw Lamp, his face now hardened, and his hand in his pocket, starting to stand up. He nodded off and dreamed sweet wet dreams.

Jimmie had gotten a nose and was fighting to keep from shooting the stuff when he got busted for a traffic warrant and went to the county jail. He ran into Fass Black at breakfast.

"F.B.!"

"What it is? What it was? What it 'C' like Cuzz," came the coded greeting. Two big, buffed, beat-up artists sat on either side of Fass Black. Jimmie took a seat on the other side of the table.

Fass Black was doing 60 days for assault. He said he could have beat it with a lawyer, but the original charge was assault with a deadly weapon, so he copped out to a public defender for the lesser charge. He needed to air out for a while, anyway, and the County was cool.

"I heard lots about you F.B. The Carips are spreading like a house eating wild fire in the Santa Ana winds. I guess every set on the East Side is claiming Carips, huh, Homey?"

"West Side too, Cuzz. Crippin' is in. We're grabbing all the territory in town and the cops really don't know what's happening. Los Angeles belongs to us, Cuzz. But, you down, Jimmie. You know what's happening. You're one of the original Crips." Everybody's ears at the table perked up at the street-sacred title.

"Yeh, Cuzz," said Fass Black, "this dude, Jimmie, is O.G., an Original Gangster from the original set, 107 Hoover Crip."

Jimmie felt uncomfortable with the notoriety. He just wanted Carole to come and bail him out. He didn't want to have to get down with any of these bucks in the County.

It turned out he had nothing to fear. Fass Black or Ray Ray (as everybody now called him) and his Crips were running the County. They even had some of the guards in on the drug traffic. Ray Ray arranged to get Jimmie into his cell. They reminisced and when they had finished, Jimmie told him about not being able to stop tooting and losing his hustle at the gambling joint because he was nodding off on the dice. Now, Carole was acting crazy, again. When Jimmie happened to mention Lamp, Ray Ray jumped off the bed.

"Short, brown-skinned, hard as old folk's toe-nails?"

"Yeh!" said Jimmie.

"Yeh, I know him. The big SMACK (heroin) man from Kansas City. He's selling almost all the SMACK in the Jungle and beginning to spread out."

"I never knew he sold it. I know he uses it like a vacuum cleaner," said Jimmie.

"If that is your partner, then you're partners with a snake. That dude is trying to Bogart every racket in town. If I catch him east of Vermont, he better be on his knees begging. He deals in heroin and P-C-P, and I don't like neither one in my 'hood. I'll bet he set you up. What have you got that he wants?" probed Ray Ray.

"I don't know. He's always been straight with me. He even gives me my drugs free," said Jimmie, his mind going back to that first experience with Smack and Lamp's face when he held up the panties.

Carole never came to bail him out, and it was 10 days before he got out of jail. When he opened the door to his apartment the morning of his release, he felt good. He had not been high the whole time he was in jail, and he felt rejuvenated. He was 19, and for the first time in a while, he felt it. He had put on a little weight and it agreed with him. He had always been tall enough, now, he was starting to buff up.

He wanted to sneak up on Carole from the back, but when the door opened and that sickening smell of PCP hit him, he could have cried.

Carole was up to Genie's apartment Tanya informed him, and little Jimmie lay asleep on a sheet on the floor, his dirty diaper next to his bare stinking behind. The apartment was a mess, roaches everywhere. All of a sudden, the door flung open and a wild woman appeared.

"Where are my damn cigarettes? Tanya, if you smoked one of my Kools, I'll kill you." She flung things everywhere, then noticing Jimmie.

"So, you out, huh? Well, what did you think I was going to do while you were in jail? I ain't had no money or nothing."

"You had money to buy that lye(PCP)!" Jimmie screamed back, asserting himself.

"No, I didn't," she said trying to cry pitifully. "If it hadn't been for Genie, I wouldn't have had nothing."

"What did you give him in return?" Jimmie shot back.

It took him 3 days to move Carole, Tanya and the baby back on the East Side in an apartment on 109th and Main. Carole was starting to come around, but Lamp had a hold on her. Even when she stopped using P-C-P, he wasn't sure she didn't still sneak up to Lamp's apartment during those three agonizingly emotional days.

When Ray Ray got out of jail, Jimmie asked him to help him set up the hit. They waited a few days for Ray to get the feel of the streets, again, then they took two carloads of gangsters to Lamp's afterhours club on the Crenshaw strip one morning after the customers had left. Jimmie shot him, then they stripped him naked and set him afire.

'Wow!' Jimmie thought, 'there's one part of him that's going to burn a long time.' As they were driving east on Vernon, they looked back and saw the red flames begin to lick their way into the wood frame of the building.

"Let's call the fire department when we get to Western," Jimmie said.

"Naw, Cuzz, that's messy. Let it burn. I don't care if it burns up the whole West Side," grinned Ray Ray. All of the Hoover Crips in the car thought that was very funny.

Chapter 5
Crip Crazy

Things were going pretty well for Ray Ray and the Crips until he had to pull his 60 day bid. Crips had sprung up all up and down Hoover. There was a good sized set on 69th Street; there were the 59's and fast rising Five Deuce. Eight Tray Hoover Crips had joined with Eight Tray Gangster Crips and formed the largest Crip set in the city. But, Rolling 60 Crip, the first and greatest West Side Crip gang (they claimed), had gotten into a shooting war with Eight Tray Gangsters.

So, Ray Ray decided to move down off Florence and Hoover to establish the soon to be infamous 74 Hoover Crip Gang, to put out the fire between R.S.C. and E.T.G and to bring East Side and West Side Crips together, again. He took Bear, Li'l Jay Stone, and Hard Times and they soon took over the streets around Florence and Hoover. They were set up in an apartment house on 74th and Hoover across the street from Brother Charles' Ice Cream Store.

Brother Charles had been one of the most feared gangsters that Los Angeles had known in the 1940's when he singlehandedly shot up the Newton Street police station after a bunch of cops beat him up. He had been a member of the notorious Boozy gang before he converted to Islam in the 50's. Nevertheless, he gave it all up willingly and totally because he was a true Believer. He loved to tell the story of how Islam had saved his life. He considered himself one of the original Muslims in Los Angeles, having converted when Malcolm X came to Central Avenue in 1956. Charles, Michael Saahir, Charles Huda from Chicago, and Captain Edward, the Jefferson High football star, had soon mapped out portions of the community for converting and set to converting. Whenever Ray Ray or any of the 74 Hoovers came into the store, he lectured and tried to proselytize them.

"Now you beat that boy all out in the middle of the street in the broad open daylight. What do you think will come of it? You gone make his family hate you."

"Naw, Bro. Charles, that was William's nephew doing most of that. William is using P-C-P and coming home terrorizing. His wife said he needed cooling down. That Angel Dust will make 'em go crazy. Give me a triple dip of that blueberry cheesecake. It ain't got no hog in it. Does it?" jived Ray Ray.

Yeh, Bro. Charles was close to 70 but hard as a rock. He liked the old man. He felt protective of him. That was an odd feeling, for Ray Ray. As the Crips grew and his power and authority got greater, he began to feel protective of more and more people. He didn't care so much what happened to him anymore, but he wanted his people to feel protected. Los Angeles was being taken over by crime, and the police could no longer control the streets. Gangs were going to be the strongest force on the streets of L.A.

"Look, Ray, I see what you're trying to do with your gang, but there's just too much hatred out in the streets. Everybody will turn on you. The police want to get you worst of all.

"Look, give it up, Ray. I'm telling you that Quran on that wall can save you, now. I know you're a great one when it comes to fighting for what you believe in, but you need help when it comes to fighting the devil. You need Allah."

"I know what you saying is true, Old Man, but right now, nothing can stop me. Not even the devil. He's let it go on too long. Now, there's just too many Crips, and we rule at night, right or wrong. And, if he tries to put us all in jails, we'll take over the jails and the streets, too, cause there's too many of us and we're growing every day. Every kid in South Central L.A. wants to be a Crip."

Ray Ray was walking out of the candy store feeling refreshed at having gotten the last word in on Bro. Charles, but he didn't understand what he saw happening on the streets. Everybody seemed ready to break up into their own little army. You really couldn't put it on individuals. It was like so many Crip gangs were becoming enormous that they all wanted to rule, and nobody wanted to accept anybody else's leadership. The streets seemed about to break out into nuclear war. He was the only one who could bring East Side Crips and West Side Crips together. Even he didn't know if he could put Rolling 60's and Eight Tray's back together, and, now, Hoovers and East Coast Crips were shooting it out. Maybe Bro. Charles was right; he might die trying.

The ice cream was good and clean tasting. He felt as though it was good for his body. He had started seriously driving iron in the county jail on this last bid, and he was more and more conscious of being fit. In fact, he would crash the pad now and see if Bear wanted to drive some iron.

The phone rang as he walked in the dingy one bedroom apartment. It looked like a motel room except for the refrigerator. There was no stove. The phone was the most important piece of furniture in the place to Ray Ray, and he considered it his alone.

"Get the phone, Ray. It's ringing all over the apartment," said Bear, a hulk of a 19 year old, who was named simply because of his ability to be ferocious.

Ray just picked up the phone and turned his anger for Bear into the receiver.

"Who is it? Well, what's up, B-Dog? Sure you right. No kidding. Thanks, Cuzz.

"Come on, Bear. We gotta get movin' Cuzz. The police found Jimmie Black's .357 magnum at the scene of the killing. They put out a warrant for him. We better go see him before they do."

They drove by and picked up Jimmie on Figueroa. He was glad to see them because it always made him look good on Fig to be seen with Ray Ray and Bear.

"They found your piece, and you didn't even tell me you dropped it, Jimmie," Ray Ray said fast, lifting the seat to let Jimmie into the backseat of the Cadillac coupe.

"Give me your strap, Jimmie," Ray Ray said matter of factly. It was a hit. The windows were all up in the Cadillac, and the air conditioner was humming, but the radio was turned down, and Ray was talking too carefully. He was measuring Jimmie for the hit.

"I ain't holding, Cuzz. Why don't you just drop me off at the police station, then, Cuzz, cause I ain't scared. I'm playing crazy, the nut's role, about the piece cause I had gloves on, and they only knew it's mine because they took it when I got busted for warrants and had to give it back. I'm saying it was stolen. Straight like that, huh, Cuzz?" Jimmie prayed they believed his hastily conceived lie.

"Don't never snitch on a Crip, Cuzz," said Ray. Bear pulled over and let Jimmie out.

Jimmie didn't really drink alcohol, but he walked straight into the nearest bar and drank a double shot of 100 proof bourbon to cool his pulse down. He walked out of the bar, immediately after he finished the drink. When he came out of the bar, it was 8:00 at night, and the August heat had broken. It was a cool, comfortable night, and the Los Angeles sky was that beautiful (but eerie) violet color that catches everyone's attention. Jimmie looked up the street at the corner of Florence and Hoover. He had reached a fork in the road of his life, and his choice now would make all the difference.

Chapter 6
Legitimate Failure

Jimmie and his family moved, bought a house. It was an excellent deal, nice neighborhood too, on a cul de sac behind Fremont High School. Jimmie had $5,000 (he was planning to buy a car) stashed. He decided to try it with the legitimate world.

"I need a job, so I decided to come and finish my high school requirements at night. I need 3 classes and the Topics test," said Jimmie to Jackie Jones who was acting secretary at the Fremont Adult School, and doing a pretty good job of acting until now.

"Jimmie, you finishing up, huh Cuzz. You know I always did like you, Jimmie, if you could've been legitimate."

"Then don't Crip talk to me, Jackie. I need a job, and I need to put my past way behind me."

"You can work here, unless you killed somebody, or something. How's your lady? Or, should I say your OLD lady?" Jackie wanted to just bite his ego. The way she and everybody in the Class of '71 at Locke had begged him not to drop out, and now, he was looking in her eyes trying to figure her out.

"Baby, Baby, Baby! Baby, Baby, Baby!"

"I like the old tunes," she said turning down the radio on her desk and snatching 3 forms. I know everything about you but your new address and new telephone number."

"I don't know the phone number, yet, either. Use the old one Jackie. Here's my new address and birth date. Have you got any counselors that might be able to help me out? I might have some problems at first -- money being the most pressing one." He wished he could hammer it into her brain cause he knew Jackie could help him if she thought hard enough.

"You can talk to Mr. Barker. He's the best, but he's the police, so be careful."

"Who else?" Jimmie said kiddingly. "Hey, what is this slavery or something? I just need a job, maybe in security or something, legitimate money. I'm a man with a family to support."

Mr. Barker turned out to be putty in Jimmie's hands. He got him a job working security part time at the school and showed him "the right look" to get over. He let him make money painting and doing maintenance with his weekend business. All the people at the night school remarked that he was a model employee.

The legitimate life was a front to Jimmie. He wanted it for his kids, especially little Jimmie, but he didn't believe it was meant for himself. He had been accustomed to having a lot of money and couldn't understand why everybody (himself in particular) didn't make a lot more money for what they did.

In fact, it was only recently that he gave up all of his street games, and he had been working for over 6 months. Carole and the kids were still on Medi-Cal, and he didn't want his next baby to be born on Medi-Cal.

"What you trying to wear me out, Baby? I'm doing my best to keep up with you, but you know you can't take our your frustrations on this," Carole said lasciviously.

Their bedroom was just like they had always wanted it. Everything was soft. They had a big king sized bed (that Jimmie had traded his old car for), satin spreads, and silk sheets that they had been given as wedding presents from their street friends. However, they had gotten so they held each other, but they thought of other lovers, nobody in particular, but it certainly took the shine off being in love.

"Jimmie Jr.'s smart and talks about his daddy, his daddy, so much he makes me and Tanya sick. I wish you'd tell him that I am his boss, and he is only 3 years old," she said half seriously, half pleadingly, but that boy had done too much stuff.

He had learned to climb the avocado tree in the backyard, and he had learned to fall out. He could bring her avocados that were low on the vine or had fallen on the ground, but he would eat them, too, and some would be nasty (cats had gotten to them first). It was like you had to watch him every minute of every day. He was so different from Tanya, who just had to have her fast pants whipped once and awhile.

"When can we get another car, Jimmie? This house sitting is getting to me. I'm fighting it, but the soaps are starting to pull me in. 'The Young and the Restless' is getting good. I know you don't wanna come home and have me make you wait to see if Dick finally gets down with Jane, do you, amigo?" she flaunted her high school Spanish.

"Ustedes quiere un caro," she continued.

"That ain't it," he said, memory straining, and they argued. They filled a lot of the time up with arguing, too much, it seemed to both of them, but they couldn't solve it. Neither one of them really thought they were intended for each other, but they were the best either could do at this point, flaws and all.

Carole thought she needed an operation, or was going to need one soon -- a serious operation. Her OB-GYN doctor had told her that she was having too many cysts. She was going to have to lay off birth control, and she was determined that she was not having any more babies. She hated being fat and pregnant, and the pain of having a baby was like death.

Carole knew she should go back to Dr. Brown, but she, also, knew what he was going to say before he gave her the advice or medicine that she wanted.

"Mrs. Black, you and your husband are blessed to be a couple that's going to have a lot of babies. Your menstrual period is a week. Relax and enjoy it. If you fight your nature, your body will fight you back with all the forces of creation."

She could picture him tall, confident and, oh, so cute. She bet he could do some natural forcing, not that she was looking for that kind of "trouble" lately, but...

"I need some pills, and I want to go see Dr. Brown." She knew Jimmie would go along if she mentioned Dr. Brown's name. "Give me $50."

"Tell Dr. Brown I said don't get rich too quick," Jimmie said as he watched what he liked best about Carole sally out the door. "Here. Here's five more dollars. Take your daughter. I'll babysit."

Jimmie Jr. had been in the back room where he had been forced to stare at cartoons by his sister, but when she prepared to leave, he was escaping on her heels.

"You're staying with me, Jimmie. You and me are going walking and talking."

It was Friday and Jimmie wasn't working for a change. He liked to take his son up to Fremont and show him the track that he had won a race on when he was in 8th grade at Horace Mann. Little Jimmie could run. He was going to be fast, too.

"You got any sprinters, Coach?"

"Jimmie, Jimmie Black! I haven't seen you in a month of Sundays. No, none as fast as you. I bet you can run 10.9 in your Nikes."

"Ten nine. That's not fast. I ran 10.5 in junior high school."

"That's yards, Jim. It's 100 meters, now. Things have changed in lots of ways since then. Heard you dropped out of Locke," Coach Morris said half querying.

"Yeh, I dropped out, but I dropped in right here at Fremont at night," Jimmie said proudly. It was funny how he wanted to be doing good for Coach Morris.

"This is my son, Jimmie Jr. He's going to win the Olympics in a few years."

"Fast, huh?"

"Like his daddy. I'll send him to you when he gets old enough to work on techniques," Jimmie flung the comment over his shoulder as he walked through the middle of Fremont High School like he was the principal with his son at his heels.

He was going to get little Jimmie a haircut, some breakfast, and find out what was going on on the streets.

Jimmie pushed Jimmie Reed on the jukebox, then The Whispers, and The Young Hearts. The Golden Shears Barbershop had records that no other jukebox had. Jimmie had to come at least once a month to play Jimmie Reed.

"Cut Li'l Jimmie's hair first, Johnny, and maybe I'll get one afterwards."

"Big Boss Man," wailed Jimmie Reed, "cain't chu hyeah me when I caw?"

Li'l Jimmie leaped in the barber's seat, but wouldn't stop squirming when Johnny tried to tie the huge barber's cloth around his neck.

"Can I slap him? Can I slap him?" said Johnny half seriously while holding him with one hand and raising his other threateningly. When he had visibly put big fear in the 3 year old's eyes, he addressed Big Jimmie. "Jimmie I ain't heard nothing about you on the streets. They stopped asking questions about you at your old apartment house months ago.

"The dude was a slimeball heroin and P-C-P dealer. Everybody that knew him was glad to see him die. The cops don't have time to look too hard. They got to try to keep up with these young Crips. They killing somebody every night. They killed..."

"Yeh, I know. I heard at the school. They shot a girl on a bus stop, coming from church last night. Seemed like it was an accident," interrupted Jimmie.

"Sure, but the police had better be looking for them, and forget about finding somebody that did the community a favor.

Anyway, since you started keeping your hair cut and shaved all that junk off your face, they see you and don't see you. If you've got anything to worry about, it's one of Lamp's Kansas City hit men friends sliding in on you," laughed the barber.

"I'm not worried. I'm hard to find for their kind. I stay off the streets at night and out of the street life altogether. How's Fass Black?" continued Jimmie.

Johnny became suddenly concerned with the precision of cutting his little customer's part. He grunted and played as if he hadn't heard the question over the hum of the electric clippers. When he stopped for a moment, Jimmie asked again.

"How's Fass Black, Johnny?"

"You mean Ray Ray, Jimmie. Don't call him Fass Black, anymore. He doesn't like it. He carries a bear around with him, and he'll sic him on anybody for almost nothing. Johnny remembered vividly how Ray Ray had gone off on him for not knowing his new name, and Bear had broken his mirror when he asked for the money for Ray Ray's haircut.

"Ray Ray's still doing okay," the barber remarked bitterly. "You know he'll never have to do without on Hoover long as he lives... long as he lives, that is," he said finishing little Jimmie's haircut.

Jimmie needed to hustle something. It was just in him to make fast money. Jail was something he knew he was going to have to experience sooner or later. People like him always had.

Maybe a woman, a real swift one, but that's hard to do without putting out a lot of emotion and time, and it just didn't come natural anymore. He had gotten so, he wanted sex to count for something more than that. He even had gone to church -- once.

It was funny, but Carole had talked him into it. The church had this big picture of Jesus, and he was like dead on the cross with an arrow through his red bleeding heart on the outside of his chest behind the preacher. The preacher seemed to be pretty much for the right, and he was obviously satisfied with everything but the building fund.

He did say a couple of things about Jonah and the whale and a man's duty to God, but it was mostly a blues teaching. Jimmie tried as hard as he could, but when they prayed and all he could see when he closed his eyes (no matter how hard he tried) was that picture of the white Jesus, it pissed him off. He opened his eyes and tried to clear his mind. The preacher was thumbing through his Bible looking for scriptures. He looked up, and their eyes met. It was a stare of mutual understanding.

The choir started on cue. But, on the way home, Jimmie and Carole argued.

"The bottom line reason why I don't want to go back to church is the effect it has on Jimmie Jr. We haven't been praying to a Caucasian god in a long time. I don't want my boy coming up thinking God is white, cause He's not," said Jimmie. By the time she had introduced him all around Greater Gethsemane, he knew she owed him an opportunity to get it off his chest.

"Are you through," she said, the kids climbing obligatorily into the back of the '72 two door Delta 88. "Are you damn through. Cause you are just 20 years old and don't know much about raising kids. At least I'll admit I don't know, but a lot of those old ladies in that church do. You ain't got no momma, and I ain't really got one. Somebody's going to have to tell us some things.

"Oh, yes, but you a Muslim, right. That means you believe in having a lot of women, huh? You can't even pray like a Muslim. I can't keep waiting around for you to do for me. I have to do for myself and you, too, most of the time in some things."

"That ain't it," he said, feeling like he had gotten his face slapped good, and they argued about things that weren't so important.

Jimmie decided he wasn't going to pick up any ladies, but he was still mulling over it one day when he ran into Fast Eddie from Fremont Class of '71. Jimmie decided to ride with him in his new, strawberry-red Seville. The women were hanging out of cars screaming at them by the time they went under the bridge at the Florence exit of the Harbor Freeway. There were two cars of broads trying to force them over. They barely got in the left lane to make the turn on Figueroa.

"Pull out your gat on 'em, or you won't make the turn," laughed Jimmie. "Stop floor showing, dude, I'm concerned about getting popped."

"Gettin' loaded?" said Eddie playing crazy and super cool.

"No, going to jail, Fool."

"Aw, don't worry about it, dude. Everything's cool. I just had this ride two days and I wanna take it on the streets. You get flack from broads just walking down the street. Now, you and me got a ribbon tied around us. How you like it?"

Words ceased between them as they came upon her. She was there, everywhere.

"I know you're not hustling, lady, not in that beautiful dress," Jimmie heard himself ply. She turned like an actress.

"Why is that? You the police? You are not the police are you?" she said.

Her brassiere was in disarray. She had that hungry look that the pimps all looked for. So, they picked her up and road her. Fast Eddie put her in the front seat, and Jimmie climbed into the back. Eddie was on her macking the pimp game hard, but he wouldn't go for a sale. She finally got pissed off and announced that she was a police, flashed a badge, and demanded that they take her back to Figueroa and drop her off.

"You sure could make a good ho for a policeman," said Eddie, snidelike. He was pissed himself.

"Excuse me, but don't put me in it. I didn't say a word. In fact, Eddie let me off here on 76th Street soon as we get off the freeway," groaned Jimmie, trying to act as nonchalant as possible.

"No, you and your wise guy friend, Fast Eddie, here might as well ride over two blocks farther and stop at 77th Street Police Station," said the policewoman, all of a sudden, really angry and with a pistol in her hand.

The police had found Jimmie's warrant for the murder immediately. It was so matter of fact, somehow, Jimmie was conned into thinking things were worse for Fast Eddie whom they kept having to slap while they tried to find something on him. 'Wow! he was probably going to miss some days at work.'

But, as the magnitude of what had happened to him began to come into focus, he wound up staying up all night. He had called Carole, and they agreed all she could do was wait until morning, then get a lawyer.

They had to sell the house quick. Everything they agreed on was so emotionally charged. Li'l Jimmie awoke crying. He could hear him crying in the background because his mother was crying.

"Crying won't help nothing. Baby, it'll be all right," he heard himself say.

The next night after being transferred to the County Jail, he had been raped and almost broken. He had wanted revenge so badly. (Worse than he had wanted revenge from Lamp.) He thought about it again, all night long.

He had a couple of choices. He could play tough and look for some homeboys who would back his play. It was easy enough. He knew who he wanted to kill, not that he felt that he could ever get back what they had taken from him, something so secluded inside him that until now he had not even been conscious of it, but it was precious. It was like forcing a virgin. It didn't make her a slut, but there was a virtue lost and replaced with a dour sophistication.

His hatred, the absence of which had always separated him from Ray Ray and the rest of the O.G.'s, was now, full blown like a bright red flower in his chest that craved blood. Yes, he knew he was a killer, now, the thing he most admired on the streets, but there was something else that accompanied this new special hatred. It was dread. It was the expectation of punishment. He was being drawn into the cycle of pain. It was a dilemma.

Of course, he could play it legitimate, do his time, try to get all the soft jobs in prison. Try to get out quickly by making friends with all the authorities. Play the light skinned, non-threatening role. He had enough Caucasian blood in his veins to dupe even the whites that hated the sight of blacks. He knew the role well, harmless and helpful. The only thing wrong with it was that other "H" -- homosexual. If he played that role, could the authorities protect him? He couldn't make friends with the other prisoners, so he would be a target. He couldn't take being raped again. He weeped quietly, and, of course, it didn't help.

Then, for the first time in his life he sincerely asked God to help him. He didn't want to close his eyes because he didn't want to just beg a white man. There were plenty of those right here in jail who thought they were gods and couldn't even get a better job. He kept his eyes open, filled with tears, and he said with all the sincerity in his body,

"Oh, God, Allah, Jehovah. You know who I'm aiming this prayer to. You know you, but I don't know you, so I don't even know what you like to be called, but I know I belong to you, and I want to stop doing wrong and start doing right. Help me. Please, help me."

Chapter 7
The Resurrection

Tehachapi was the hottest place that Jimmie had ever been. He remembered being in the San Fernando Valley in an August heat wave two years ago and thinking that people could not survive in that heat without air conditioning. Tehachapi was like that all the time, and Jimmie almost never felt air conditioning in the almost six years that he spent there.

On the other hand, reflecting, he could truthfully say that almost all that he had learned of worth in his 25 years had been learned in those 5 years in prison.

His righteous education started with Wash, his first cellmate in the joint. Jimmie had planned to size up his cellmate and everybody else at Tehachapi before he made his decision about how he was going to do his time. He liked the fact that Wash was smaller than him, although he was old, somewhere in his early forties.

"This your first time in prison, huh, jitterbug?" said Wash, hoping he sounded confident and jail hip.

Jimmie didn't say anything, at first. 'Was the guy trying to say he was soft, a mark?'

"What, have I got a glass forehead or something?" replied Jimmie.

Wash laughed, "Naw, li'l brother, I'm sorry if I insulted you. My name's Ali. I come in peace."

It was a perfect match, Wash (who was changing his name to Ali because he loved Muhammad Ali), the semi-legitimate street hustler who had never been a real father to his son, and Jimmie who had never known his father, but, now, at 20, needed protection and guidance more than at any time in his life.

Hour after hour, Ali would talk about the streets of Los Angeles. From Watts to Baldwin Hills was his territory. He had been born in Watts, raised on the East Side off 45th and Main, went to Catholic high school, Mt. Carmel on 70th and Hoover, and married a society chick who insisted they had to live in Baldwin Hills close to her family. Ali's daddy was one of the biggest black contractors in the state, and Ali had inherited his persuasive talents.

He had scoffed at college and gone straight into sales after high school. He bragged that he could sell anybody anything if they had the slightest need for it, and everybody from Baldwin Hills back to Watts seemed to want (if not need) everything they did not have. Jewelry, clothing, household items, cars, books, insurance, and securities, he had sold to individuals, stores and at concerts and festivals. The kind of goods made no difference. He would look in the people's faces, work his way past their defenses and into their hearts, then sell them. He was known for carrying big wads of money.

"Everything you see was sold by somebody, Jim. The highest paying profession in the world is sales. There's some books you gotta read. The World's Greatest Salesman and How to Win Friends and Influence People. You'll never have to worry about money," said Wash, his mind going back to how amazed and proud his father had been when he made $5,000 for the down payment on his house in a week at the age of 19.

"Yeh, I know," came Jimmie's somewhat unconvinced retort, "especially if you sell dope or women."

"Neither, Brother, not since I became a follower of the most honorable W.D. Muhammad," and the 5'6" Wash stood a little taller. Then Jimmie knew why he wanted to be known as Ali.

There was a fine Muslim community at Tehachapi. The brothers had their own mosque, or room for prayer and teaching the word of Allah. They bought books, papers, pies and were always organizing monthly affairs for the wives and visitors who began to flock to the tiny prison on the outskirts of Bakersfield.

Jimmie took the shahada, "La illaha ilallah, Muhammad dar rasullallah," (I bear witness there is no God, But Allah, and Prophet Muhammad ibn Abdullah who brought the Quran 1400 years ago is the last Messenger and seal of the prophets of Allah).

Jimmie, who could read but seldom read, began to read voraciously. He took Malcolm X who read and rewrote the dictionary while in prison as his model, and Ali was his personal tutor.

He was astonished at the secret knowledge in the books. The people he should have known about and didn't know: Garvey, Elijah, Adam Powell, DuBois and the perspicuous W.D. Muhammad, etc. It was a paradox. He was in prison, but he had never been so busy. He couldn't wait to get back to his cell and read. The books and conversations with Ali were constant water to his swelling brain. Some prisoners agonized their time -- doing years in seconds. They fought each other like penned up dogs and days were grueling in the summer's awesome heat and lonesome the balance of the time.

Jimmie's body was in prison, but his soul was, for the first time, free. He studied Quran and slowly the light of it began to glimmer in him.

He was a trusted and helpful prisoner, more valuable to the operation than any one guard or clerical person on the staff. The warden viewed his soon approaching parole date with the chagrin he felt at losing any other of his most valuable staff.

Jimmie had mastered every aspect of the office work in the small administrative facility located on the compound, and used his clerical opportunities to plan and promote with Ali's assistance the monthly Muslim talent and cultural showcases that were becoming extravaganzas that everybody at the prison looked forward to (inmates and personnel alike) it eased the burden of the routine.

Though prison was a very productive place for Jimmie, it was a boiling pot for most of the other prisoners and prison personnel. There was a constant struggle between the prison gangs: The Mexican Mafia, the Aryan Brotherhood, and, now, (as Jimmie remembered Ray Ray had predicted) the newest and most volatile gang, the Consolidated Crips. Death was always one false move away in the prison if the top blew off the tentative peace.

Jimmie, Ali, and the rest of the Muslims stayed outside of the deadly politics, being more involved in expanding the religious freedoms of Muslim inmates. In fact, sometimes the killing of an inmate or the outbreak of protracted violence between the gangs would cause some of the African Americans to convert. There were even two Caucasian Muslims at Tehachapi who had escaped the meaningless cycle of hatred and violence of prison life.

Jimmie had no visitors the whole time he was in prison. Carole had really had hard times since he left. She had been forced to sell their house to pay the lawyer's fees, and she had moved back into an apartment on 109th and Main. She didn't have a car, so she could not drive up to see him, and things were so tight, at first, that she didn't want to buy bus tickets for herself and the kids, then, come back and have to do without until her next welfare check came.

She had a little job working days at Winchell's Donut Shop, but her welfare check was adjusted for what she made, and working was barely worthwhile. They wrote each other almost every other day when he first came to Tehachapi, but for the last year Carole had not written very often often, and when she did, the letters were short and said nothing about what was happening in her life.

Once, Jimmie had called and talked to her, but the conversation was strained. She seemed listless and distant. At first, he reckoned that she was losing patience, which he considered natural. He told her that he was bound to be released the first time he became eligible for parole, but he didn't think she believed him, probably shielding herself from the, now, expected great hurt in her life.

Jimmie knew he owed Carole a lot. She had taken him in when he was only 10 years older than her daughter and saved him from the streets when he was old enough to leave the last of his foster homes. She had loved him and taken care of him when the world had shown him its butt for as long as he could remember. She had consented to have his baby (though she would probably not admit it), Li'l Jimmie Jr., who was why he really wanted to get out, now.

Somebody had said that Jimmie Jr. had gotten himself shot. He especially wanted to see about that. He knew he couldn't allow his son to be misused, let alone abused. His son would be shrewd, and bad news for anybody who thought they could abuse him.

Jimmie wanted his son to go to Horace Mann and maybe John Burroughs Junior High for the last year. He knew Jimmie Jr. couldn't go to Locke or the 'Mont, so he figured Washington for high school. That's where it was going to be in control, anyway, and Coach Morris was there, now. He was going to have to start making a legitimate living, but this time he knew why because he knew what he wanted, now. It was freedom. He first realized he knew when he read a poem called "Sympathy," by Paul Laurence Dunbar, "I know why the caged bird sings... when his blood is red on the cruel bars .... "

The metaphor was too perfect. He saw it, oh, so clearly everyday except when there was an extravaganza, and they were only stint hours in weeks upon weeks of gloom. He knew what freedom was, and he wanted it. He could say it to himself. He wanted it for himself and Jimmie Jr. Freedom was free from jail and the fear of jail, and Jimmie knew that he would have that once he could get out of Tehachapi, "Sittin' on a pea waiting for it to hatch."

"Jimmie, you got any money," Ali said, the cigarette smoke curling into his eyes.

"Money? Are you kidding? I came here broke and got broker. Why all of a sudden you need extra money all the time?" Jimmie heard himself say, knowing Ali was smoking and drinking again. 'Trying to get ready for the streets,' he called it.

"I just need 2 dollars, Jim, unless you holding it for something real special," shot back Ali.

"You can have what I have," said Jimmie, tired of the banter. They both knew that they were working for the cause of Almighty God Allah. What did pennies matter? His homeboy, Ali, was getting out in two weeks, and it was almost as if Jimmie was getting out himself. He felt so good for the brother. He was going to join Ali in a few months, taking for granted, of course, he would make parole on the first time.

"This is a crap game," Ali announced, his hands deftly fondling the dice. "Everybody that doesn't understand the game, please stand back and let the players play. I am the houseman. I cut all snake eyes, ace and deuces and boxcars." Ali was making a killing, but he had rationalized it. If he didn't take it, they were just going to spend it on cigarettes and booze. Unfortunately, his reacquired substance abuses were beginning to take most of his winnings, too.

Ali was the highest ranking prisoner in the laundry and had access to all three shifts. Every time somebody in the laundry turned over, Ali had another pidgeon.

"Spread out from the wall so everybody can see. You must hit the wall, gentlemen. Later on if there are any players in the house, we'll spread out a blanket, and you can shoot your best shot." The game hardly ever stopped. Ali would commission inmates to run it for him when he wasn't there. If you worked in the laundry, and you didn't gamble, you would have to learn because, not only was Ali taking everybody's money, he was the only person who could show you how to get paid in the laundry.

He had written every African American senator, representative, and mayor in the state, and a few from other states. His father had taught him that every man respects a letter written in your own legible handwriting.

His dad, Milton Washington, Sr., had taught him so much. Unfortunately, he had also taught him to gamble.

"Take that you, G.D.M.F'ing dice," the youngsters said sweating bullets, having just gotten to the joint. He seemed to think if he threw the dice harder, they would do what he wanted them to do. They never did, as they would slowly come to rest. He was losing badly, and he was messing up the game. He started saying the game was locked and raising all kinds of sand. Ali thought a little crazy youngster they called Taiwan was going to be the one to tear this wild new youngster's head off.

It was getting hot beneath the press of the machines and the freshly pressed sheets. The new youngster seized the dice again and flung them against the wall maniacally, stood up, pulled his pants half way down his behind, and sang:

"Not just saggin', I'm blue raggin', Don't you wanna be like me?" Taiwan's jaw slackened.

"Crip here," said Taiwan, and they turned on the other crap shooter and Ali and robbed them. It was such a bold play. They had to kick Ali almost senseless before he stopped coming back on them.

"What is it Washington?"

"It's two youngsters on my third shift, Captain. I think you are going to have to put them on some other duty," Ali said, hoping his emotion wasn't too evident.

"Who are you talking about?" said Cpt. Shauwecker. "Who are we talking about, here, Washington?" repeated Shauwecker glad to help because he and everybody else knew the laundry had never been so efficient as it was since Washington took it over.

"It's the new kid, Taiwan, and the burly one they call Mad Dog," said Ali, relishing his revenge.

The prison was caught up in a lightweight controversy. Was Wash (as everybody had started calling him again) right to go to the warden on some kids that had probably just caught him cheating? Old con's mulled it over slowly, as most prisoners took sides.

Wash had kept the Muslims out of it by not attending meetings since the incident, but he knew that Jimmie was his strongest help. If he ever needed to play the card, it was an ace.

The new youngster, Mad Dog, had called all the Crips out on the dispute, and it looked as though they accepted him as their fiery new leader. Surprisingly, many of the newer prisoners were Crips from South Central L.A., and they started behaving real roguish, staying in trouble with the prison authorities. They sent Wash the word that they were taking over the crap game in the laundry.

Wash had become real cold and paranoid. He reasoned that all hell could jump off in the crap game at anytime, so he hid some iron poles under the pressers and instructed certain people on each shift as to what to do if it went down. Wash and his people kept arming themselves and arming themselves until it got so everybody was hoping it would happen on their shift.

Jimmie was vaguely aware of what was going on. Wash had some sort of plan, but he wanted the Muslims to stay out of it. What worried Jimmie was that if something happened between the Crips and his friend, he didn't know if he could keep the Muslims out of it.

Wash was walking around like a little general, now. His chest was all swollen out with his plan for total revenge and his short release date. Even prison guards, secretaries, and other lower personnel look somewhat longingly at a prisoner who is about to be released. Seldom do they leave whole, but it's even more admirable to see one leave proudly, as Wash was doing. Then too, some of the prison personnel were jealous.

"When I came here, I was going to rotate before Washington, but he's leaving 6 months before me," Warden Haynes said, his face reddened with frustration and the 3 martinis he had at lunch with Mrs. Wilson, his third voluptuous secretary since he arrived at this hot as hell hole, Tehachapi.

"I think he brags to the other prisoners that he was embezzling 3 times what I make. He's got a crooked laugh," ranted the warden.

Mrs. Wilson looked at him, pitiably. He was a royal fool. She'd do what she had to do, but she cared more about one of these prisoners than she did about Warden Haynes and his freak self.

"What it is? What it was? What it 'C' like, Cuzz," Jimmie turned instinctively toward the familiar greeting. It was Li'l Jeffrey from the 107 Hoover set. Jimmie had not seen him since that night on Fig.

"What that 107 Hoover Crip Gang 'C' like," Jeffrey continued. He was no longer small. He was 6'4 and buffed with a beautiful black sheen.

"Ain't you Skinny Jimmie from the Original Hoover set?"

Jimmie couldn't deny it, and at the same time he was happy to see somebody from the old neighborhood.

"Li'l Jeff, hate to see you in here, but it's good to see you," they hugged.

"How are you doing, Brother? Are you handling prison life, yet? asked Jimmie, genuinely concerned.

"I'm having a few problems, Jimmie. It ain't nothing I can't handle. There's a lot of homeboys from L.A. here. How you been doing Jimmie? Everybody on the streets says you're going to make parole on the first time. That's beautiful. All the O.G. Hoover's respect you for what you did, and how you stood up for Ray Ray. You know they still can't touch him," said Jeff, looking around to make sure no one was listening.

"Much as 77th Street L.A.P.D. has tried," laughed Jimmie.

"Ray Ray is okay. He said to tell you that they brought him in the station and told him that you squealed on him, but he just sat there and looked at the light. He knew it was a lie."

"Hey, Jeff, I know you didn't know Carole, my lady too well, but she's staying over on 109th and Main. Have you seen her or heard anything about her?"

"Naw, Jimmie," Jeff lied. Why give him some grief behind a broad. He knew his little Criplette, Cassandra, couldn't wait for him.

"I did hear your son Li'l Jimmie got shot. It might have been a funky deal, too, Jimmie, so you might want to look into that when you get out. You know HCG is backing your play," the inference was obvious.

"Thanks, Jeff," said Jimmie heading towards the library.

"It's Mad Dog, now," came the proud reply.

When Jimmie came back to the cell later that night, he found Wash doing pushups.

"You need to rethink this revenge thing, Wash. You've gotten even, and you've got a lot more to lose..."

"Even. Them young bucks almost kicked my brains out, and you think getting 'em kicked out of the laundry is going to even things out? They even threatened to take my crap game away from me. Well, when they try, I'm going to spill some of their blood this time," raged Wash, jumping up from the floor.

"Did you ever stop to think why our religion says mercy is greater than justice," Jimmie replied. "What happens if it gets back to the warden and the parole board that you beat up on a fellow inmate with an iron pipe, and you have also been running an illegal gambling game for the last 3 months.

"I know you think you're old and have all the sense, but listen to me. These Crips are not going to roll over easily. It might take the guards and everybody else to make them stop fighting. You might have to kill one or some, and you might win the fight and lose your parole. Even worse, Wash, why you want to get caught up in that cycle of hatred with those young brothers? They're just victims striking out blindly at society for the funky hand it dealt them. You taught me that when I first got to the joint."

The next morning Wash walked over to the table where Mad Dog, Taiwan, and some other Crips were sitting. When they saw him coming, they tensed, but he patted Mad Dog nervously on the arm with the dice hidden in his palm.

"Take 'em quick. They're yours," said Wash. "Don't make them your religion, though."

Warden Haynes and the guards busted the crap game 3 nights later. Everybody who was caught was faced with the maximum penalty, an extra year, for gambling.

"I thought I had him, damn it, Mrs Wilson. I knew I had him," moaned the warden. "I know that's his crap game. Why wasn't he in it?" He continued, talking actually to himself.

"Maybe it wasn't meant to be," she said belligerently. She was just about to tell him where to get off.

When Ali came back to the cell after his shift, he woke Jimmie and told him about the warden busting the crap game. He started to thank Jimmie, but before he could...

"Don't thank me, Wash. Thank Allah. He's the one who keeps giving us all chances."

"Allahu akbar," said Wash.

"Allahu akbar," repeated Jimmie and both of their faiths were strengthened.

Chapter 8
The Homecoming

The streets were not the same when Jimmie returned to L.A. They seemed to smell differently. When he dismounted the bus at the terminal in downtown L.A., there were beggars everywhere. He didn't remember that before. It was 10 o'clock in the morning, and on every corner, in every nook stood a beggar. They rifled the trash cans for food.

Skid row had seemed to be only a small strip of Los Angeles Street east before he left as he recollected, but, now, the bums had spilled all over downtown Los Angeles.

The legitimate people had changed too. They were colder. They walked briskly to avoid conversations, and everybody avoided eye contact. He had never felt particularly comfortable downtown, but this was even worse, almost eerie. He had been in town almost an hour and spoken to no one except for shaking his head, "no," and waving off the beggars and zealous merchants. Jimmie walked over to Spring Street and caught the Number 7 heading to South Central L.A.

He headed straight for the back of the bus. The pungent smell hit him before he could sit down. It had been over 5 years, but the smell of P-C-P was unmistakable. Somebody was awfully bold. Jimmie didn't want to be there when the police came, so he decided to get off at the next stop. He was starting to get a little frantic.

"Wanna buy a joint, Cuzz?" the youngster sitting in the corner of the bus said with nothing approaching covertness. The people on the bus paid little attention to the acrid aroma coming from the rear of the bus. They opened windows, which helped very little and the bus driver never looked back.

Jimmie shook his head at the youngsters, still not having spoken. He dismounted the bus and walked back to the Greyhound bus terminal to catch a cab. No sooner than he arrived and began to scan the cabs parked out front, when...

"As Salaamu Alaikum wa rahmatullallah," came the clear greeting. The words refreshed him. He turned, replying "Wa Alaikum As-Salaam, Brother." He recognized an older brother whom he had seen all his life, and never known, Bro. Less Muhammad.

"You look good, Brother," said Less smiling his unmistakable smile. "Where are you going? Need a ride to the Southside?"

Jimmie was, "Yes!" to all of that and, "Yes!" to "Would you like to stop by the mosque and school to make salat?" They went down Santa Barbara (now called Martin Luther King Blvd.) east to Central where the old Elks Hall was shining like new money in the L.A. sun. As they were leaving the huge, richly carpeted, salat room, Jimmie realized it was noon, Friday, time for Jumah prayer. Almost immediately he heard it clear as a bell and scintillating as a soul sister.

"Allahu Akbar, Allahu Akbar."

They had been so happy at Tehachapi when Bro. Nashid from Bakersfield had been allowed the right to have Jumah prayer service in prison, and, now, he was amidst a literal sea of Believers, young and old. The children were streaming down two opposite stairways in the lobby, hurrying to wash and pray.

"This is what I wanted to show you," said Brother Less, and they smiled at each other and turned around.

It was mid-afternoon before he stepped out of Brother Less's cab in the, now, faintly familiar neighborhood. Jimmie, really, wanted to see Jimmie Jr. Where would he be? He was almost ten, but he couldn't be too far from the apartment house. He had to be home from school by now.

He gave up. His natural urges came upon him like the pull of the earth's core. The thoughts he had been forced to blot out of his mind were real and on the other side of the apartment door. He had practiced this 25,000 times in the last three weeks. He didn't bother to knock, just pushed open the door, saw Carole standing with her back to back to him, engrossed in KGFJ-AM. His eyes got real crafty as he tipped up on her, his fingers and palms crying out in lusty anticipation.

Though everybody -- Carole, Tanya, and even Little Jimmie Jr. -- seemed to be going through the motions of life, Jimmie was ecstatic with his new freedom. The great burden of prison had been lifted. Anything else was a light load. "No problema," as the Latino brothers say.

When Carole had gotten switched to the graveyard shift at Winchell's, Jimmie made her quit. It solved a lot of problems. The phone soon stopped ringing off the hook on the weekends.

"It's funny," Ali had said once as they lay in their bunks. "Our women are more obedient and caring when you treat them badly than when you treat them good." Ali had been reflecting on his marriage when it came to him.

Jimmie had not been amazed. He was aware of it especially in his relationship with Carole. Before he went to prison, however, he had no compunction about treating her badly. Nothing would make him more appealing to her than another woman's interest.

Jimmie had resolved himself to continue to, as Ali so aptly termed it, "engage and disengage himself in the services of a paramour" for this very reason. But, now, it was clear to him that he could not do this to her.

"So you back, huh, Jimmie Black?" said Jackie Jones, now, the full fledged secretary at Fremont Adult School. "Come into my office." When they closed the doors to the confines of Jackie's office, she turned on KJLH-FM and began to reminisce.

"I knew you had a felony of some sort 2 days after you enrolled in night school, Jimmie. I know you think I'm a fool, but I wanted to see you graduate, so I protected you," Jackie said offering him a cigarette.

She was beginning to get fat in the right places, and she wore a tasteful, loose fitting African style shift.

Jimmie refused the cigarette, but Jackie accidentally dropped the pack, then leaned over quickly exposing her large breasts for a fleeting second. He didn't want to hurt her, but he knew this was trouble. Bells and sirens had been going off from the moment she had closed the door.

"You know I'm Muslim, now," he said.

"That means you want a lot more babies," Jackie said.

"Yeh, but like you told me once, Jackie, legitimately."

Jackie had been married and divorced since they had seen each other. She had a 2 year old daughter, Du Shon.

"I've got an 9 year old son, Li'l Jimmie Jr., and a 16 year old daughter."

"Yeh, I've seen Jimmie Jr. With my luck, Du Shon will probably fall in love with him."

They wouldn't let Jimmie work security because of his prison record, but Mr. Barker got him jobs doing maintenance and painting on weekends, and Jackie gave him the best gift of all, his high school diploma.

Jimmie saw the bold calligraphy on the paper and he felt like he had graduated from U.C.L.A. He couldn't help it. He had to kiss her on the cheek. Fortunately, she was behind the counter in the main office -- they both had to lean.

Jimmie really didn't want to work for anybody during the week. He wanted to sell. He was selling wholesale meat and fish at first. Then he started selling clothes that he bought from the garment district. It was like Ali had said. You could sell anything they had the slightest need for because they wanted everything they didn't have.

Jimmie hadn't seen Ali since he got out of prison, but he knew it was only a matter of time before he ran into him at the mosque on Central Avenue, "Felix Bilal". The old brother had taught him a lot that was true about sales and life. Jimmie wanted to let Ali know about his plans.

In only a matter of a short time he would have a get-around van so he could deliver fish and meat. Then he was going to buy a piece of the rock. A piece of this East Side land for him, his wife, and his babies (and of course he was going to have several more).

Carole straight out refused to come to the mosque with him. She was still on welfare and paying most of the bills. When Jimmie talked about having another baby, she said they were too poor, though it wouldn't hurt her county check any.

The one bedroom apartment was a definite problem. You could clean all day every day (which Carole rarely did), but it would still look dirty and junky. The faucet in the sink in the bathroom did not work, so water had to be dipped from the tub all day long.

Jimmie couldn't pray there. There was no privacy, and he couldn't study because of the constant competition between Tanya's ghetto blaster and Carole's 24" color console.

Since Carole was way beyond subtle suggestions, and he wasn't beyond subtle suggestions, and he wasn't making enough money, yet, to demand a change in their lifestyle, he stayed out of the apartment as much as possible and didn't pressure Carole about Islam.

He wanted to take Jimmie Jr. with him to the mosque, but after the initial thrill of having a daddy had worn off, the boy was distant and secretive. Worse than that, Tanya and Carole seemed to alibi for him.

"How's Jimmie doing in school?" queried Big Jimmie.

"He's doing all right, now. They don't call about him getting in anymore trouble. What you expect? You know what old folks say, 'The apple don't fall too far from the tree," she jived.

"I went back and got my diploma. I did graduate from high school," he said, immediately wishing he hadn't said it.

"So what? A lot of people do. So, I guess you can get a job as a judge, now, huh?" she snapped.

Jimmie knew that this could break out into a loud, senseless argument, so he left it alone because Carole had begun to say he thought he was better than them.

He had wanted to go to Jimmie's school and check on him, but Carole said Jimmie was on the free lunch program and when she applied, she didn't mention a husband, so she didn't want the county kicking her off for any reason. That had stuck in his gut like a twisted rusty knife, but he had told himself to be patient.

He had talked to the kooky guy down the street who had shot Jimmie Jr. -- Mr. Crenshaw. The guy was real nervous and sweating profusely when he said he was Jimmie's daddy.

"Your boy was looking through my bedroom window at me and my wife," Willie Crenshaw said with more anger than he intended. This guy had just gotten out of prison for murder. He looked nice enough, but it was obvious this guy could handle himself.

"All I can tell you is what I told the police. Your son was stealing my garden hose and he must have heard my wife and I making love, so he sneaked a peek. I really don't think he saw much because I got a glimpse of him, and he ran. I thought he was a man, so when he jumped from behind the car, I just reacted. You know, I was in Vietnam."

Willie continued implying he had combat experience which, though he was in Vietnam, he did not.

"Anyway, I immediately realized it was a kid and went to help him. My wife called the ambulance, and I guess between us we saved his life. And, that's the god's truth," Willie said beginning to get caught up in the memory of his bravery and humanitarianism.

Mrs. Crenshaw looked out her kitchen window and shook her head. 'Why had she chosen to marry this lying poot butt?'

Big Jimmie stopped short of thanking Mr. Crenshaw for shooting his son. He was hardly taken in, but it was pretty clear that Jimmie Jr. was stealing. Why had he been doing that? Mr. Welfare had taken care of everything so well to hear his wife tell it.

Chapter 9
Jimmie Jr. Goes Back to King Hospital

Jimmie Jr. awoke to the smell of alcohol and the sound of ping pong. If things were quiet, sometimes, he could hear the ping pong game in the soundproofed recreation room -- it never stopped. Jimmie liked it most because it was the doctors' game. Sometimes he would beat one rushing through the halls to console some impatient patient. It made him think like a doctor, but he probably wasn't as good as he used to be. He never knew the doctors by name. He tried to remember their faces. Some he liked, and some he hated. He lay in his bed trying to remember the mean, tough doctor, the one who he hated most for putting him out the hospital last time. He hoped he didn't have to see that dude again.

"What are you doing back in my hospital, again, young man? I'm going to have to start coming to visit you at home, so you can stop coming here to visit me. Oh, you're awake," she stopped smoothing out his sheets and started taking his pulse and trying to put a thermometer in his mouth. Jimmie turned away and smiled at Nurse Shelley, his play mother.

"I didn't wanna get shot again," he said almost truthfully.

"You weren't shot. You just reopened your wound, Jimmie. You're going to have to let yourself get healed completely before you scramble under cars and stuff like that. Most people never get shot, but when they do, it takes a lot longer to get well than you took. We're going to have to keep you here longer this time, Jimmie." She smiled, and Jimmie fell in righteous love for the first time.

They wouldn't let him play ping pong for a week. He had to admit, though, he really didn't feel like it until Saturday, but that first game was like heaven. He only played twice (he lost and had to wait a long time for his next turn), but knowing that you were going to play ping pong was the only reason for looking forward to tomorrow.

Otherwise, it was meet every moment head on, expect problems, and try to make the most of things. In fact, ping pong was the only thing that made him want to live to be 10. That and being O.G. someday. Ten years old use to seem so far away, but, now, it wasn't so old. He felt old though.

"You can't forget that you're just a little boy, Honey. Your momma says you won't even hug her when she comes," said Nurse Shelley.

"I didn't feel good. My side hurt," he lied.

"You hug me all the time, Jimmie. Don't try to hurt her. She feels guilty enough. When she comes, today, I want you to promise to be nice. Hug her or don't try to hug me anymore. I mean it."

Shelley tried to sound piqued, but she understood why Jimmie didn't like his mother. She was a b .... She flirted right in front of her husband, and she acted like she was sorry Jimmie had not been shot again. She was so proud of how bad he was. She bragged in her pathetic storytelling when asked and sometime she volunteered her bete noire anecdotes.

Jimmie Black Sr. was something else, however. It was obvious where Jimmie Jr. got his good looks. His father was tall, thin, fairskinned and handsome. He wore his hair real short, and she guessed he was a Muslim. But, Little Jimmie's mother sure wasn't anything but a Watt's witch.

"As Salaamu Alaikum," said Big Jimmie as he came into the hospital recreation room where his son was playing ping pong. When they got another house and a little dough, he was going to buy Jimmie Jr. a ping pong table.

"How you doing, Son?"

"I'm okay. Wal kum Salaam," Li'l Jimmie fumbled with the Arabic, his eyes fixed on his ping pong game.

"Don't talk that mess up in here. I told you to wait till I checked things out. You ain't even suppose to be here. You ain't on my Medi-Cal card," Carole whispered loudly, acting as if she were doing something surreptitious.

"Hey, look, woman, I'm talking to my son, and that's my religion. And, it's going to be his, too, as soon as I get him out of here." Jimmie had finally lost his patience.

"I don't see why we can't talk to Jimmie at his bed. I don't like it in here, all these people. Jimmie Jr., let's go back to your bed. I wanna sit down," said Carole.

Begrudgingly Jimmie Jr. gave up his game (even though he was winning 15-12). He was so embarrassed at his mother. She had her hair up in pink rollers with a scarf, some Jordache jeans that were too tight, and a halter top. Her navel stuck out on a roll of hairy, fat stomach. She smoked cigarettes nervously even after the security guard told her not to. She argued with his daddy, loudly.

"I hate this damn Watts. If we had some money, we could have Jimmie transferred to Cedars Sinai," Carole said trying to put down the nurses and act as if she was too good for Watts.

"I like Beverly Hills. I'd get my hair fixed if Jimmie was in Cedars. No telling who we might see in Beverly Hills, huh, Jimmie?" She tried jealously to recapture her husband's attention as father and son walked ahead of her hand in hand.

"So you Crippin', huh, Li'l Jimmie? I understand, but we need to talk. We just have to talk about it. That's all, man to man."

"I don't care what that policeman said. My son ain't no damn Crip, and don't you say that no more. I'm doing all I can. I thought he was going to school like he should've been doing," said Carole whimpering, but not for Jimmie Jr.

"How do you feel, Li'l Jimmie? You look pretty good. Nurse Shelley says you don't get enough rest," said Big Jimmie as he helped his son into the clean white sheets.

"I ain't tired no more, Daddy," the word was new for him and kind of clumsy, still, he was beginning to like saying it in front of other people, "and I like to play ping pong," he blurted out, immediately sorry to have opened up and shown his feelings.

"Don't you get out this bed, you little fool. You just gonna make yourself worse. Now, say something smart like that to me. I'm gonna show you who's the boss."

Jimmie Jr. started yawning and feigned like he was dozing as his mother continued to chastise him. Shelley watched Mr. and Mrs. Black leave, arguing. One thing was for sure. Mrs. Black was loaded off something.

Jimmie's days in the hospital were the best of his life. Except for the almost daily embarrassing visits by his mother, his father (who wasn't so bad), and sometimes Tanya, Jimmie was having a vacation that could have hardly been better.

Nurse Shelley was even more attentive than before. The food was good. He didn't have to worry about clothes, and his ping pong game was becoming outstanding. Nobody seemed to be rushing him out of the hospital this time either. He loved pretending Nurse Shelley was his mother. It would be great if she married his daddy.

"Jimmie, do you know what child abuse means?" Nurse Shelley said.

"Why you ask me that?"

"Does your momma beat you, Jimmie?" Shelley blurted out.

"Yeh, I guess so."

"Do you love her?"

"No," he said quickly remembering how she called him "the world's biggest problem", and how the older boys kidded him about her big behind. No, he didn't like her (he wasn't really sure what love was). He hated his momma and Tanya, too, but why did Nurse Shelley want to know that?

"You're leaving, today, Jimmie, but only for a little while. You've got to go to a hearing with a judge, Dr. Cohen and your social worker. They want to decide if you should be taken away from your mother," said Shelley.

Jimmie wondered what she meant. He liked Nurse Shelley, but he didn't always know what her words meant. Was she trying to do something good for him? Maybe she wanted him to be her son. He could dig it.

It was like he had two mommas -- one he remembered holding and crying on her breasts. He loved her breasts. They were so soft and comfortable, but, this new momma he hated because she hated him.

He really wasn't sure that he wasn't adopted or something. This lady, who called herself Carole and hated him, couldn't be the same one he remembered so fondly though vaguely from his infancy. Carole had hit him with a hot iron, and he would never forget. She would kill him if he didn't watch out for himself.

She had tried to make him call a lot of men daddy, but he wouldn't. It was hard for him to even call his real father, daddy. It just seemed so young sounding and scary.

Big Jimmie was his daddy, and that was going to be great. He had gone and scared Mr. Crenshaw for him. He wasn't even too scared of Mr. Crenshaw anymore, since they told him his daddy had scared the neighbor everybody disliked. Ol' Mean Mr. Crenshaw hadn't even stared at him the last couple of times he walked past. Now was the time. He would hit up his wall as soon as he got out of the hospital.

"He doesn't pay attention very well," said Dr. Cohen, interim staff psychologist at Martin Luther King Hospital. "I've got to do a fast report on this kid for a D.P.S.S. investigation, but I can never get him to talk.

"Young man, do you have excessive pain where you reopened your wound?" continued the doctor, constantly sizing Jimmie up.

Jimmie had found out quickly that if he tried to answer the doctor's questions, it would lead to more and more questions, and sometimes his answers were no good and "not thought out", so he rarely spoke to this one. He knew from experience that if he didn't encourage this particular doctor, he would go away.

"Nurse Tabor, you have amazing communication with young men. Please be so kind as to play this tape and explain the questions so that little Mr. Black will respond. Then fill this report out. I'm sure you can have it for me by time for the hearing this afternoon. I have the utmost confidence in your ability in these things."

Dr. Cohen's mind was on his apartment units in escrow. He would just ask for a continuance at the hearing so he could have a long talk with his real estate broker. He was going to try to drag this case out, anyway. The decision on custody would be made based on his recommendation. Maybe it would get picked up and covered by some enterprising newspaper reporter as a prototypical case in the mayor's policy change vis a vis Watts.

"Anything else," Nurse Shelley said a little more ambiguously than she had meant to.

"No, just stand by and at ease. You remind me of my army nurses," he laughed. It pleased him that he was still attractive to women, though women were forever in his, now, faint but painful past. He tried to swagger for her as he left.

"Girl, you still trying to catch that Caucasian. I swear he's a fairy. I done tol' you. He's too cold." Edna had old eyes from nursing almost 30 years, but she fancied herself in possession of 20/20 vision in spiritual sight.

"Look Edna, I need a man, and you know any other young unmarried doctors besides Dr. Cohen and that new resident -- who, by the way, I am going to nail," said Shelley hungrily.

"I hear you, girl. I have seen him, and can I help you in any way?" said Edna.

"Just throw me a victory party when I catch either one of them, cause I'm gonna get me one," swore Shelley.

"Can two big dogs whip a little one?" Edna grinned. They slapped hands in the hallway that housed the tiny nurses' station.

"What's Dr. Cohen going to recommend for Jimmie, Shel? You know it's about time for that baby to have to leave."

"I think he wants to recommend a foster home for Jimmie. You know, Edna, I think he's doing the right thing for the wrong reasons. He really doesn't like Jimmie, but he hates the sight of his daddy. Jimmie will be better off away from his momma, though." Shelley fanned her face with her hand.

"You mean the Watts Witch. That broad needs to dig herself. She comes to the hospital loaded and makes a scene every time she comes. I guess that's why the boy loves this hospital so. That and your tender loving care.

He loves you, too, Shelley. Don't you wish you could keep him?"

"Kind of, but he's too big. I never would get a husband, Girl. I want to have my own baby, and husband, and condo, and Benz, and..."

"And boyfriend on the side," teased Edna.

"Well, maybe," said Shelley smiling as she gathered up her tape recorder and forms and headed to the recreation room to interview Jimmie.

By the time Shelley finished with him she knew every nasty thing he had ever done and with whom he had done them. She didn't seem to think they were so nasty though. Every bad thing that he had ever done she blamed on his mother which was fine with Jimmie.

Shelley said the judge was going to ask him most of the things she asked, so he might as well try his answers out on her. He was glad when they finally finished, and Shelley said he could go play ping pong until they sent for him to go to the hearing. It scared him, however, when she said she wasn't going with him.

"But, you'll be all right, Jimmie. If you get scared, just stop and think, but if you get confused, say you don't understand, and everything will turn out great," coached Shelley, and she gave him a big hug and waved as he and the social worker waited for the elevator.

That afternoon when Big Jimmie came to the hospital alone for the first time to see his son, he had not been informed that Li'l Jimmie was to go to a hearing to decide upon his custody. The magnitude of what was happening made him tremble in the air conditioned hospital, though it was late August.

"Can they take Jimmie Jr. away from me and Carole, Nurse? I don't see why anybody would wanna do that. Can't I do something to stop it?"

"Not that I know of Mr. Black. I think the problem is you and your wife haven't done enough for the boy up to now. Who's to say it's going to get better in the future? Jimmie openly admits to hating your wife. She's repeatedly physically abused the child, and so have you. That, coupled with the mental anguish she causes him, has driven him to the street gangs.

"You wouldn't believe the number of boys we have coming in this hospital with bullet wounds and the number that die. In my opinion, Jimmie would have a better chance in a nice foster home." Shelley was livid. She had worked herself up when she wrote the report, and she felt that she needed to dump it on somebody. Mr. Black was just as bad as his wife as far as she was concerned because he put up with her.

"You don't really understand," Jimmie began, haltingly, flabbergasted at the pretty nurse's emotional outburst. "I... I just recently got out of prison. I know my boy's been neglected physically, mentally, spiritually and any other kind of way you can think of. When I first had Jimmie, I didn't know anything about being a father because I was young and dumb, but I'm changing all that, be it the will of Almighty God, Allah."

Shelley didn't hear another word that he said, though he continued in his slow singing kinds of phrases. These black men were so pitiful. He seemed sincere, but when the judge heard that he was recently released from prison, it was sure that he wasn't going to release Li'l Jimmie to his father's custody, even if he left the boy's psychotic mother.

Well, he could just persuade his sweet heart out, but she would never give another black man her faith and trust.

Jimmie could see it in her. She had been bitten and beaten. When she was very young, she had probably wanted the mountains around her, but, now, she wanted skyscrapers, having flung her soul at the feet of one black man too many who put the pedal to the metal and burned rubber on her sincerity. What had he to offer her? His infidelity? They both loved Jimmie Jr., and each doubted the other's motives.

"You think Jimmie's better off without me? Don't you know that what he needs most is a man in his corner?" Jimmie was fighting his own bitterness.

"Do you know a man, Mr. Black? You probably don't even have a job. Your wife's on welfare. Don't you think I know Jimmie's here on Medi-Cal?" Nurse Shelley seemed to be enjoying putting Jimmie in his place. After all he had tried to pull that heavy guilt psychological trip on her.

He probably figured she was from the West Side and square. He would be surprised to know that she had fought her way off of Figueroa and worked her way thru college -- Cal. State, L.A. She had been married, too, if you wanted to call it that. But, she had learned to read most black men, and the poor, pitiful, East Side ex-convicts were her special hatred. Most of the poor babies who came to Martin Luther King Hospital in Watts had daddies in prison or dodging prison.

'Well, Mr. Jimmie Black, Sr., I hope they take your son, and everybody who looks like your son, and daughter. Making a baby sure doesn't make a daddy and Shelley would tell that to her own daddy, if she ever saw him again.'

"Just because I don't have a job that you respect, doesn't mean I don't work, but I doubt if a judge would understand or even approve of what I do. I sell things on the streets, and I have a peddler's license to do it. Don't ask me how much I make because about all I could tell you is that it's more and more every month.

"No, I can't take care of my family right now, in the way welfare has made them accustomed to, but I have two things that are worth more than your big fancy paycheck. I've got a family and strong faith. I'm still working on patience, so I better leave before I say something mad like you want me to say. Then, you could have the proof that you want. Then, you could say without a doubt that I'm nothing just like you thought. Just like your father and maybe your brother, but for sure, like your last black lover. As Salaamu Alaikum," he said as he headed for the elevator.

Shelley seethed, but she was certain that afternoon the court would claim Jimmie Jr. as a ward based on Dr.

Cohen's report which she had virtually written. The social worker on the case would substantiate the accusation that Mrs. Black was often drugged and incoherent. Li'l Jimmie's recent conflicts with the law and subsequent hospitalizations were evidence of parental neglect.

Jimmie Jr. understood little of what the judge and the others kept asking him if he understood. He thought when they asked him if he would like a new mother to take care of him that they were talking about Nurse Shelley. But, when the judge asked his mother where was his father, and she said his daddy didn't care about him, it struck him that his daddy was being lied on. If he was here, his momma Carole wouldn't say that.

Why wasn't his daddy here? Maybe he didn't care what happened to him. Maybe Nurse Shelley didn't care either. Why wasn't she here? This was really an important meeting. What if they took him away from his house? Maybe that might not be too bad. His family would probably consider themselves better off -- except his daddy. Big Jimmie was something like he wanted to be, strong and smart. His mind reeled. This is important, he thought...

"I gotta go to the bathroom," Jimmie Jr. said, whispering loudly, impatiently to Dr. Cohen.

"No, he don't," said his momma, roughly. The psychiatrist was going a thousand miles an hour in another direction. He turned, deftly, interrupting an intense discussion with the judge.

"But of course, Jimmie. It's only down the hall that way."

The judge impressed with this smart, efficient young Dr. Cohen, shifted in his chair and paused in his listening. Everyone in the comfortable little chamber began to chatter among themselves. At first, about their opinions regarding the case, but, then they lapsed into their discussions of the latest tragedies, unprecedented atrocities, etc.

Jimmie turned straight into the elevator as it opened. He hoped it would close quickly because he also knew that his momma would be on his heels. Suddenly, as the doors began to close, he saw her rush out of the doors from the chamber. He moved to the corner of the elevator, so she couldn't see him.

"Jimmie Black, Jr. if you are on that elevator, I'm going to whip your b... !!" The doors finally shut and it was finally starting to descend. He thought he saw her flustered face, but he was not sure.

He had meant to run off so he could think, but this elevator ride was the greatest. It was like a parachute. Oh, he hoped it didn't stop. He clutched on to the walls in the corner. It stopped, slowly, feathery. The door opened and a young woman entered.

"Lady, how many floors in this building?"

She entered alone.

"30, and I'm going to the 29th. Wish you could ride with me." She smiled and wondered who this attractive youngster belonged to.

"I'm Jimmie," he said immediately feeling comforted by her warm smile, "but, I wanna ride up all the way without stopping," he continued boldly.

"Let's ride this one then," she said as they crossed the hall and waited in front of the express elevator doors. The doors opened and an older Caucasian secretary stepped out.

"See you after lunch, Gale," said the older lady.

"Don't you hurry back, Mrs. Stein," said Gale charitably. Then she and Jimmie climbed onto the elevator as if it were a rocketship.

"Pilot to co-pilot," said Jimmie, "push to the top."

Gale pushed 29 and they began to sail. He had quite a time riding the elevators. It made him feel a whole lot better. When he thought about his problems, it was much more clear.

He didn't want to live with his momma because that's who he was always running away from. He could go and see his father when he wanted to because he knew he would be selling stuff up on Imperial.

It was strange the way his daddy made him feel. It was almost like he felt when he was up on the lot on Fig with Termite and his Crip Crip partners. Like you had some protection on the street. All kinds of big problems never came up. Even the merchants in the stores didn't treat you rough. But, it was because they knew they had better not.

"What goes around comes around, clown." He remembered seeing Termite point his finger in the man's face who ran the Avocado Corner Market.   Next day, **TERMITE 107 H C G** was all over the store's walls. It was like an artist had written his signature and secret signs on the business.

Yeh, you didn't mess with a Crip, and he was a CRIP. If they asked him anything else, he would just tell them like Termite said to tell them. "I'm a Crip, you fool. Crip here!"

That would make them leave him alone. But, they had to catch him first, and he stepped on the mat to the automatic door and walked out onto 1st Street in downtown LA. It was the first time he had ever been downtown. He just started walking downhill.

When he saw a street sign that said Broadway, he felt better. He didn't know where he was, but Broadway was one of the streets he knew best. Even if they didn't have his other streets, he could keep coming back to Broadway, and when he got ready to go home, he would just walk up Broadway that way.

Downtown Los Angeles was great. There were big fruit stands and people selling food on the street. All you had to do was look hungry and ask, and some people would give you a peach or nectarine. He had $2, but he didn't want to spend it because he might have to take the Broadway bus, and he didn't know how far he had to go to get home.

"Que paso," said the Mexican American boy. He was about Jimmie's age, 9 or 10.

"Que paso," mumbled Jimmie trying to sound confident. He had heard the term before. His mother would say it to all the Mexican men, and they would smile back, but he better give this dude a question to answer while he sized him up.

"Crip here. What set you from?" said Jimmie.

"This White Fence," said the young Mexican pointing to himself and posing.

"What's a White Fence?" Jimmie said.

"What's a Crip, fool? You don't know White Fence? The Fence is all over this part of town, gringo, p... What's a Crip?"

The words came out fast and cool. Jimmie was reminded of Loco Jojo. The dude in the neighborhood who they said had Mexican in him.

"You don't speak Spanish, huh, Bro? That's cool. I thought you was a cholo for a second, Homes. Maybe a little 18th Street or something come down here to try to take my hustles, but you are all right."

Jimmie knew he and Flaco were going to have to fight because the dude kept trying him. They boxed and wrestled as they weaved their way in and out of alleys and stores. They got money twice, once in a candy machine coin return, and once they took this package to the post office and mailed it for this cook at an outdoor hamburger stand. One thing for sure, Flaco knew how to hustle.

"I've got to take this money home, Jimmie. You can come with me if you want. My sister and my family don't speak much English, but it'll be cool. Later on we can come back downtown and play video games at the arcade."

It sounded so good. It was like Magic Mountain or something he had heard of and longed to do when he was older and finally had some guts (intestinal fortitude he remembered his father calling them). And, here this S.A. (Spanish American) took it for granted. What did he have that Jimmie did not know existed until now?

"Su amigo esta flaco, Flaco," said the soft brown lady in the broad opening of a gigantic white house. It was old (and probably scary looking at night) but in the bright sun it was beautiful.

Flaco had 3 brothers: Sergio, who was real big and played football for Manual Arts High; Martin, his younger brother; and a baby boy, Benjamin. Benjamin was the one that got to Jimmie. He made you wanna take care of him or watch him. The "nino", as everybody called him, couldn't get enough of climbing all over Jimmie, and the family loved the baby, so they thought it was a sign.

Jimmie couldn't believe it. By the time he had decided what he was going to rip off when he left, they had him bowing his head (but not closing his eyes) in prayer at dinner. Everybody was a Catholic, but him. He guessed he was a Muslim cause his daddy had taught him not to pray to the white god.

This new world was spinning, reeling with wonders. Maybe he would stay here a few days and then go back home. His momma for sure and maybe the police, too, were looking for him by now. He maybe should just catch that Broadway bus Number 7 like Flaco had shown him on their way over.

"El pollo esta bueno," said Jimmie getting another piece and thinking how mad his momma would look at him whenever he sat down with them to eat or dared to look like he wanted the scrawny second piece. Now, he was learning Spanish, and people were acting like they cared if he was hungry. Gustavo (Flaco's real name) was like a brother his own age.

"I like you, Jimmie, I like you," said the pretty little girl.

Celestina was 10 and sun shined in her pretty brown face and eyes. She pulled on Jimmie to come and talk to her, and teach her English. She sat so close to him while he explained the record that when she rubbed her smooth cheeks against his, an urge began to build in him like a gusher. He grabbed Celestina, suddenly, and rubbed himself against her.

"No, Jimmie," she said knowing his look. But, it was over quickly. Jimmie knew what had happened. He didn't know if he should feel ashamed. She must know, too, he thought.

His underwear was slimy and threatened to show on the elastic band of his drawers which he wore showing above his pants in the sagging Crip style, but, somehow, he didn't want her to see his business seeping out. He turned, finally, ashamed.

"I don't mean to," he said. I don't know what's wrong with..."

"Shhhhhhhhhhh," said Celestina as they began to catch the attention of the others in the spacious living room and adjoining dining room. She led him outside, and he waited for her while she left and returned with Flaco.

The sign said, "Union Ave., 800 S.", and they turned up 8th Street headed again for downtown.

The night sky was clear and dark blue and there was no chill in the air. Celestina's dark shiny hair was sprawled out over her shoulders and touching the tip of the strap of her halter top.

Downtown was buzzing with activity, and the lights made Broadway look like daytime. They hurried to the arcade with its flashing, clanging, pinball machines and video games. They first checked out the coin returns which were good for one quarter. Flaco found a pinball machine with a free game left on it which they shared, but it was fun just watching the players live and die as the silver ball bounced, or Mr. and Mrs. Pac Man ate their way through obstacles and everybody's pockets that dared defy the electronic addiction.

Jimmie was tempted to change one of his dollar bills into quarters and get his video fix to show off for Celestina who hung on to his arm, but he knew from experience how Pac Man could eat up money fast, so he held out and contented himself with watching the various players curse and brag as the arcade played its strange exciting sound. They checked the coin returns once more and headed off into the bright night.

Flaco preferred the alleys that were pitch black contrasts to the brightly lit streets. He said he was looking for his homeboys. After 3 or 4 adventures into these eerie caverns that were peopled by scraggly faced drunks so dirty that Jimmie couldn't tell if they were S.A., white, or black, they turned into an alley that beckoned to them with music before they entered.

By the time they got to the homeboys, The Temptations' "My Girl" was providing them with a loud musical score. Jimmie could hardly see anyone, but he could tell by the voices that there were a bunch of teenage girls and boys hovering around the radio.

"Chuy, Shark, Li'l Tito, how you homeboys? Que paso, hombre?" Flaco was grabbing dudes and embracing them. Everybody seemed to have a special greeting for him.

"Li'l Flaco," said El Cholo, "you look like if you keep on making money, we'll call you Gordito." El Cholo took deep fast drags of the marijuana smoke into his lungs.

"What are you little cholos and cholas up to. Myself I'm going to party at the house on Whittier. You're all invited, and let me know if you have any problems, little cholitos." he mocked as he and Big White Fence strutted out of the alley taking their music with them in huge, gleaming radios. Some wore bandannas tied around their fists -- posing and strutting toward their cars parked across the street.

Jimmie was exhilarated. He felt secure with Flaco, Celestina and White Fence. The night was almost totally upon them, though, and he knew he had better start moving toward that South Broadway bus.

Chapter X
Prayer Works

"You think I don't like Li'l Jimmie because I didn't want no nother baby, huh, Jimmie? I just am sick and tired of the pain in the butt. Wash his clothes and his snot nose. Wash his butt. When he stopped messing on hisself he started stealing and getting caught. Sometimes I think he tries to get caught. I always seem to be at school or in the police house, and you know yourself Jimmie, I ain't had much help raising him.

"My momma won't even take him for a weekend, anymore, and you good with him, Jimmie, but you ain't been here lately, and I thought you was going to die in prison after I heard they raped you in the county, cause you was a Crip when you left, and..."

Jimmie was hurt by the realization that he could not blame Carole the way he wanted to. He knew he was going to hit her, and that had been his great dilemma while he waited for her to return from the custody hearing.

He had almost resigned himself to giving her a good shaking when the psychiatrist's office called and asked if Jimmie Jr. had returned home. The police had then come and searched the apartment for the boy almost apologetically. Surprisingly, they seemed caught up in the humor of Jimmie Jr.'s daring escape and frolic in the courthouse.

Big Jimmie hardly saw the humor in his son being out on the streets, with no money, and maybe afraid to come home. His pulse quickened as he thought of the shaggy characters looking for a mark in downtown L.A. Now, Carole was saying she was going to award custody of the boy to the county.

"It was so easy," she said. "Jimmie would be better off if he got a good family. He was going to be a street man whatever happened.

"You know him, Jimmie, but not like I do. He ain't the kind of boy that needs a whole lot of help from a woman. He's going to have it hard keeping the women off of him. If he lets them catch him off guard, they'll make him weak as water. Tanya and me keep him straight."

The words were so true, except Jimmie Jr. didn't have to live past tonight. He pulled on his straw hat and walked out without speaking.

"Bring him home, Jimmie. I pray he's all right. He's wearing blue Jeans, a blue shirt and tennis shoes."

Jimmie honestly didn't know if Carole meant it. He scoured the streets around his house first, the vacant lots, the school grounds, the alleys, the corner hangouts. Nobody had seen Li'l Jimmie, but almost everybody knew him. Big Jimmie talked to a lot of Crips for the first time since he had gotten out of jail, and most of them knew his son but weren't aware that they were father and son. Even Bear seemed concerned when he heard what had happened.

"Yeh, I know your little boy, J. He's the one that got shot over on Main. Sure you right. Come to think of it he looks just like you. He sure don't scare easy. That's my little partner. He gone be all right, J. If something happens to him, let me know. Me and Ray Ray will ride down on anybody mess with one of our little homies. Straight like that, Cuzz."

Jimmie could see that Bear meant it, but it didn't make him feel better to know that Li'l Jimmie was so well thought of on the Hoover set. He was moving too fast for 9 years old. Sometimes fear was a good thing. It was a protection. The fearless die young in South Central L.A.

Big Jimmie decided he was going to have to check downtown because he was almost sure his son had not come back to South Central Los Angeles. It was 10:00 P.M. and Friday night, so downtown would be jumping. He wasn't sure where to start looking, so he went to find Brother Less.

Less was at the liquor store hangout on Imperial and Broadway. They jumped in his green cab and took the Harbor Freeway downtown. They searched several arcades, and nobody seemed to have seen him, but finally an old guy making change in one of the arcades on Broadway said he had about 8 o'clock, and he was hanging with some kids from White Fence.

After Big White Fence left the alley, Jimmie, Flaco, and Celestina stayed around a little while to "jam" with the little homeboys and girls. All the music was oldies and very familiar to Jimmie. It seemed that these S.A.'s were deeper into old records than anybody Jimmie knew. Celestina, who fumbled with English, knew all the words to the Supremes' tunes.

Though he, himself, had heard the records, they belonged to the old days, and he had assumed that only old people listened to them. Jimmie liked funk music. It was Crip music to him. He and Termite would listen to Funkadelic and practice poplock, the Crip dance, that required separate movements of all the parts of the body. Poplock was fun, but it was serious business if you wanted to be a Crip. It was never done with girls.

Sometimes, he would throw a few moves to show off in front of them, but to actually touch a girl while dancing like Flaco was doing, now, seemed kind of scary. It was very dark in the alley, but he knew Celestina's eyes were asking him to dance with her as she sang:

"Love child, never meant to be.
Love child, born in poverty.
Love child, always second best.
Love child, different from the rest..."
Suddenly, Jimmie's body tensed. His muscles rippled. He ticked and wall walked in the pantomime poplock style unique to Crips. His body tensed and relaxed melding perfectly with the beat. It was like watching someone choreograph an epileptic fit. The other dancers stopped and watched Jimmie do more than dance. He was making a unique statement. It was like he was destroying all the traditions of dance and recreating them in his own rebellious style. This dance was young. It was Los Angeles, and it was innovatively American. Flaco turned the music up higher.

All of a sudden from the mouth of the alley came a deep surprised scream. The children turned and saw two large men blocking the exit to the alley. One was clutching his body and gagging screams but reaching for his attacker. The other man's face could barely be seen in the dim light, but his smile was unmistakable.

He struck his victim with his knife, knocking him down to the glass and concrete of the alley, now. The victim covered his face pitifully with his bloody hand, but his attacker was on him, stabbing the knife into his neck and face and pulling it out as viciously as he drove it in -- maniacal now in his grinning frenzy for the kill.

Flaco had long since turned the radio off as the youngsters started searching the dead end of the alley for weapons -- bottles, boards, a rock.

It all happened so fast. Li'l Jimmie wasn't even afraid until they saw the killer stab his victim while he lay on the ground. It just went on and on and on...

"Come on!" said Flaco who was leading them out armed with Celestina's stiletto. "Let's make a run for it, muchachos."

But, when they got closer, the two men were right in the center of the alley, and the knife blade dripped blood as it came up and down like a sharp hammer.

The little homeboys and homegirls froze. No one imagined death could be like this. They had only thought of death playfully. A quick bullet... not this.

Celestina screamed. It was a piercing, fear filled prayer for help. The killer's arm seemed to hear the scream first. It paused, only slightly, but missing its mark for the first time. The knife blade crashed into the concrete floor of the alley, and the madman grabbed his own bleeding hand. He turned on them.

Something pushed Li'l Jimmie out of the pack of youngsters, and he found himself standing side by side, bottle in hand with Flaco.

The madman must have been cut badly because he was jumping around and sucking his hand, but he was literally growling with anger. He was as big a man as Li'l Jimmie had ever seen, and he really didn't think all of them were going to get out of the alley alive, even though they had weapons. But, they sure were going to have to fight, or all of them might die tonight, right here in this alley.

The thought of dying had never scared Jimmie before, but the probability made him shiver. He broke the bottle quietly. Suddenly, the man charged. Flaco's knife flashed toward his stomach, and Jimmie tried to reach his face with the bottle. The knife bit his hand, but the big man just wiped Jimmie off and sent him thudding into the wall dazed.

Flaco was bouncing on his toes when the madman turned on him, again. Jimmie could see the man's broad back hovering over Flaco who looked smaller than ever, now, his voice cracking.

"Run, Celestina. I'll stick you good, now, Gringo, come on."

Jimmie knew Flaco was no match for the madman. He told his body to get up, but his head was full of pain. He threw the bottle feebly at the man. He wanted to curse and holler at him, but something was wrong with his head. He could not speak.

When the killer struck Flaco that first heavy handed blow smashing him against the opposite wall from where Jimmie, now, tried futilely to brace himself and squirm to his feet, it jumped out of him.

"Allahu akbar!"

He didn't quite know what it meant, but it was the only prayer that he had ever been taught.

Celestina and the others broke past the madman, who was pummeling Flaco with a fury. He paused as they passed, but quickly decided they could not be caught, or, possibly his madness had overcome him once more for the smirk had returned to his lips, and he was visibly lusting for the kill, again.

Big Jimmie was turning the corner to the alley, running smoothly, but when he encountered the screaming, wild eyed youngsters fleeing, and saw the figure of a man pounding the life out of a small boy halfway up the alley, his feet no longer touched the ground.

The smaller man drove his fist into the side of the huge killer's surprised face, knocking him off the boy. Then, Big Jimmie let it all hang out, all the pent up prison hatred was, now, loose. He put the toe of his black Florsheims in the big man's Adams Apple causing him to gag and grab his throat falling backward. Then Jimmie's heel came crashing down upon the huge man's pelvis. At first, there was a tenseness there, but only momentarily. Now, he could feel the organs, jellylike beneath the force of his perfect blow. The killer let out an animal-like scream and lurched backwards while on his back. Jimmie was kicking his head, now, intent upon finding the temple.

"Jimmie, Jimmie, stop! Allahu Akbar! Allahu Akbar!" Brother Less came huffing and puffing into the alley. His words had no visible effect. Less had to bear hug his much smaller friend and turn him around, so he no longer saw his prey.

"Allahu akbar, Jimmie. Don't kill him."

For the first time Big Jimmie saw his son lying against the wall, arms akimbo, watching intently, eyes wide with pride. He crouched down and examined his son quickly. There was blood coming from his head, but except for the fact he seemed unable to talk, the boy appeared to be all right.

The other youngster whom the maniac had been beating when Big Jimmie arrived was still unconscious, and the life seemed to be seeping out of him.

"Go get your cab, Less. We got to get them to a hospital."

"You're all right, now, Jimmie, huh?" said Less.

"Yeah, I'm cool. Hurry Less. Salaamu alaikum."

Bro. Less was back by the time Big Jimmie could carry his son to the mouth of the alley and returned to get the thin, almost lifeless Latino youngster. Less headed straight for County U.S.C. HOSPITAL EMERGENCY. As they drove they hardly spoke. Big Jimmie tried to focus on the scene in the alley.

There was another body of a man that they had stepped over coming out. What had happened? He didn't know or care if he had killed the bearlike Caucasian man because it was certain that Big Jimmie's victim had been doing the victimizing before the tables had been suddenly turned.

The two boys were laid upon stretchers and taken in to be examined immediately after they pulled up to the emergency door of L.A. County (U.S.C.) General Hospital.

The spectacle of two youngsters, one black/one Latino, both unconscious (though Jimmie Jr. had only fallen asleep with the weight of the days experiences), being rushed into the bowels of the hospital accompanied by the vigilant stares and apprehensive manners of Big Jimmie and Bro. Less, broke the tedium of the Emergency waiting room for an emotional moment, but when the swinging doors finally flapped closed, the motley crew of bleeding Latinos, emaciated Caucasian drunks, et al, resumed their pregnant waiting.

After an hour and a half of waiting without any word, Jimmie beat on the plexiglass window where a sleepy clerk sat behind a typewriter. She was catching a graveyard shift catnap, but the insistent pounding awakened her.

"What cha want?" She said as the slim man came into slow focus. Then, attempting to regain her tact, "Oh, 'scuse me, Honey, I didn't mean to snap at chu. Can I help you? Oh, I don't know where they took your sons. Weren't there two little boys? Oh, you don't know the other boy. Did you fill out the forms? Only for the one? Well, they'll be out to tell you something any minute now. Just be patient, dear. These things take time. Be calm..."

'One thing is sure,' mused Brother Less. 'A crime had been committed in that alley.' They had stepped over a dead body at the entrance, and when the police came, there was going to be a murder investigation, and Jimmie was a convicted murderer. In police reasoning, that meant he was going to lose his boy to the courts for sure.

The older man looked at his younger counterpart anxiously awaiting the news of his son's status. Less hoped and prayed his friend and Muslim brother could withstand the woe that he was about to face. It was the curse of South Central Los Angeles about to strike again.

The first born and sometimes whole families were being torn away from black fathers. The ritual was well worn with practice like some savage shrine scrubbed bloody with crazed passionate embrace. But, still, it was not traditionally taken for granted or understood. Yet, almost without fail, some court was standing between every black man and his babies in South Central Los Angeles.

Less, himself, had all but given up seeing his daughter born in his lusty youth and forbidden to him by the court when he was unable to muster the child support that her mother's social worker had assured him was a small price for him to pay to see his daughter. For Less, then, recently released from prison with no job and no legal skills, it was impossible.

Only in wistful waiting moments did he reflect upon her, and invariably, if he wrestled his dilemma in his mind too much, he would once again attempt to change his life and wind up drinking all day, every day, until Islam would rescue him.

"Jimmie Black, Sr.," said the nurse with no indication in her face of how Jimmie Jr. was.

"I'm him," Jimmie was unaware of speaking as he hurried to the doorway where she stood.

"Your son is fine, a few bruises, but he should be himself after a good rest, Mr. Black. But, the other boy has lapsed into a coma. Can you give us any information about his parents or where he lives?"

Jimmie had hardly considered the little S.A. youngster whom he had beaten the bearlike Caucasian off of. How had Jimmie Jr. hooked up with the boy? What had happened in the alley? He knew nothing.

"My son had run away, and when I found him, he and this other boy were in an alley. The Latino boy was being beaten up by this big guy, and my son had obviously been fighting with the big guy, too. After I got the guy off of the kid, I brought both boys straight here. Will Li'l Jimmie be able to come home with me?"

"No, Mr. Black, we cannot release him to your custody until we complete a police report. In matters of this sort, the law requires a complete investigation..."

Jimmie Black went to bed somewhat relieved, but the next morning he was awakened brusquely by the L.A.P.D., taken to jail, and charged with a double murder.

Jimmie Jr. had been in and out of foster homes ever since the judge had declared his mother unfit in a snappy hearing and he had been placed in the custody of the court and sent to Maclaren Hall.

Jimmie remembered his first days at his latest foster home. The lady was nice enough, but her husband hated him. Jimmie had sulked and brooded the first two weeks. He went to school but barely spoke. The kids were different than kids on the East Side. Everybody at Raymond Avenue School seemed to be rich (they laughed at people who ate the free lunch. It was called the "county line" and was the focus of most of the jokes in the school).

Worst of all, the fracas in the alley had left him with an unwillingness to speak. The words no longer tumbled out freely. They were awkward and required considerable thought and effort, and it seemed he never could say what he felt. He frustrated adults with his head shaking and shrugs.

In school it was considered a lack of intelligence and he was put in Special Education classes -- which the kids all knew meant dumb. Even Mr. Freeman, his foster parent, who knew all about his situation considered him dumb after awhile.

"Why don't you talk, Jim? I know we would get along a lot better if you responded once and awhile," said Bob Freeman, once again trying to make pals at the dinner table.

"He'll talk soon enough, Bobby. Jimmie's been thoroughly mistreated. He'll talk in his own good time," said Shirley Freeman, patronizingly.

"He can talk, Baby, but I think he's lazy. When I said we could keep a foster child, I didn't expect an idiot," said Mr. Freeman, ignoring Jimmie's presence.

"The boy needs love and affection, Baby. He still doesn't quite trust us. Do you Jimmie?" cooed Mrs. Freeman.

Jimmie shrugged and looked at the meat on his plate as if the act of eating was totally engrossing.

"See he won't even talk to you, as good as you treat him, and with all the money you're spending buying him clothes, we're hardly making anything out of this deal at all. What do you want, Jimmie? What do you want us to do? Just say something. Say anything."

The words came in a coercing tone. Jimmie, no longer able to disregard Mr. Freeman, tried to think so he could speak.

What did he want? He wanted to be with his daddy. He had not seen him since that night in the alley when he proved to himself that praying worked. Jimmie Jr. had never even had a chance to thank his daddy for saving his and Flaco's lives. If, indeed, Flaco had lived. He never found out. He had not seen his father since.

Jimmie's eyes blinked as the middle aged man brought his face within inches of his own. He wanted to scream it into this stranger's face.

'I want my daddy. I love him and he loves me. He's the only one that loves me.' He wanted to say, but what came out was a shy,

"My daddy. Wa-Want my daddy..."

"Your daddy!" The words incited Bob Freeman. "That's a joke. Your daddy is going to jail for a long long time. Your daddy killed two people, and he's in jail, probably forever."

"Don't," said his wife. Jimmie bolted out the door, tears bubbling up inside. He would not let them see him cry.

He came back later that night and knocked on the door sheepishly. Mrs. Freeman let him in and tried to comfort him. She understood, she said. She apologized for what her husband had said. Don't worry. Things work out...

"MAN KILLED IN ALLEY IS SKID ROW SLASHER!"
Blared the headlines of the Los Angeles Herald Examiner.

"Police have matched a blood sample of George Taravakian, a transient found dead in an alley between Hill and Broadway last month, with samples of blood found on or near three victims of the infamous Skid Row Slasher. The blood sample and composite description of the Slasher have led police to conclude that he was Taravakian.

"Lt. Harry Toma, spokesman for the L.A.P.D. homicide investigations unit, said, 'George Taravakian, killed on the night of August 12th in a melee with a downtown street gang, has been conclusively identified as the mass murderer known as the Skid Row Slasher. We have very strong evidence that Taravakian was present at three of the Slasher murders, and it seems merely a matter of time before we tie him to the rest of the 20 murders, heretofore, credited to the mass killer known as the Skid Row Slasher...' "

The news swept the county jail, and Jimmie, when he heard it, knew how the butterfly felt when the metamorphosis takes over his spirit.

"You a hero, Cuzz. You a righteous hero," said Li'l Kenbone.

Then it slowly began to dawn upon him. The reality was with him totally, now. He was again going to be freed. But, he had killed twice in revenge and with impunity. The first, a black man, but an idolater and adulterer, a malicious killer, but, still, a man from his own tribe whose life had ceased at his hand.

Jimmie Black was a killer's name, and he vowed to never own it again. From now on he would be known as Yusuf Bilal.

And, now, the most impossible inner city irony had made him a killer once more (though overwhelmed with revenge for his son). This time he had even killed a Caucasian, nevertheless, he was again to be freed. It strengthened his faith in Allah. It strengthened his faith in America.

If he could do this, what obstacle could stop him? He would go after his dreams. He would go to college then teach. He would some day preach that there was a God, and His proper name was Allah. He had no color or race, but He was powerful, all powerful.

Chapter 11
Jimmie Black Sr. Becomes Yusuf Bilal

Ray Ray couldn't wait until his homeboy, Jimmie Black, hit the streets. The sets were alive with the story of the Crip who had killed the Skid Row Slasher downtown. The police even looked at Crips differently.

"Raymond, you're the big Crip around town. Who is this Jimmie Black? He one of yours? Guess you got a sharp one or two in your gang, huh?" said Sqt. Mutz, his face red in the L.A. sun setting beneath the Florence underpass.

The new black Captain at 77th Street Precinct, Cpt. Johnson, had put out a directive that gangbangers were to be treated respectfully, but that was L.A.P.D. Mutz was Highway Patrol, and h e had a lot of street lessons that told him never to trust a Crip. He had yet to see a good one. He used to brag,

"They are toilet tissue to me. I wipe my a-- with 'em. Every time I see one I hassle him."

Ray Ray had seen Mutz turn around into the Tune Up Shop. He had stashed his gun in the bushes off the Harbor Freeway and walked under the underpass to meet the motorcycle cop as he approached the light.

It did not surprise him. It had become more and more difficult to walk down Florence, with or without a piece. If it wasn't 3 or 4 different kinds of police hassling you, it was some youngblood (Bro. Charles had taught him to call them that) trying to play fast gun. South Central L.A. was getting to be more and more like the old West. You couldn't walk down the street without a gun.

It was generally believed that the police were dumb, but Jimmie knew that all of them weren't dumb and most were scared. They were mostly a nuisance to him.

Mutz was different, however. He was one mean motorcycle cop. The kind that would either get out or get killed, but never retire on the job.

"Check you out for smiling, Mutzah Ball. Yeh, Fast Jimmie's one of mine. I'm telling you being a Crip is divine. You can't be one, but you can do business with the organization. Come on, let me make you a millionaire, Mutz."

"Those drugs are making you crazy, Raymond. Watch yourself. I'm waiting for you to slip. I don't care what they say at 77th Street. You a criminal, and first time you do a crime, I'm going to be there making a living off of you. And, you can tell that to Mr. Jimmie Black, ni...." He twisted the epithet trying to get it past Ray Ray's guard, but the light had changed, and Ray Ray's Stacy Adams shoes seemed to sing as he crossed:

"Rhythm walkin' in my soul,

Rhyming my running, strutting stroll."

He walked into Florence Records on Broadway. All the little East Coases from Bethune Jr. High were busy feeding Pac Man's voracious appetite, but everybody stopped, and the sycophantic echo began,

"Ray Ray!"

"Ray Baby, my brother."

"Mister O.G."

"There he is, Mr. Crip, O.G. #1"

Some of them (emboldened with puberty) would nervily grasp his hand, "What it 'C' like, Cuzz."

'It felt good to be treated like a superstar', thought Ray Ray. 'Superstar? He was the founder and commissioner of the league. But, it was not an easy thing. Blood brothers had started to kill each other like mad rabid dogs.

'In fact, there were Mad Dogs dubbed in every gangster set, and they attacked without provocation, almost blindly, mostly because they couldn't handle that water (PCP) or that Olde English 800 (8-Ball). But, the blood feuds had committed more and more families to the total destruction of others.

'He had managed to keep his fingers out of the blood, lately, though i t w a s tempting, at times, but his reputation was real, based on real events, many of which had, now, become folklore.

'And, now, Slick Jimmie Black had the newspapers praising Crips. It was perfect. Now, all he had to do was call a meeting of every Crip gang in the city in honor of Jimmie Black. It was a perfect front to pull all the Crip gangs together on certain issues... codes, once and for all.

'The first problem was going to be a place to hold everybody. The best place was Pepperdine's lawn on Saturday afternoon. It was basically the 8 Tray set, but it was big and splendid, so several gangs (that were down with the Trays) felt free to drift through the vacated old church college grounds on 79th and Vermont.

'This had to be a set that drew at least 5,000 gangsters. Otherwise, what they decided wouldn't have enough impact. No, this was going to be the meeting that decided what Crip gangs were going to rule in the 80's. He would give them a focus. For the first time he would tell them what CRIP really stood for. Many thought they knew, but only a few truly knew, and of those that knew even fewer understood, and those that understood would never say. The Community Revolution was kept In Progress by only a few people, and it was the responsibility of the leaders to take ground.

'He remembered standing in front of Fremont begging Bunchie Carter to let him be a Black Panther when he was in junior high school. Everybody at Fremont, Locke, Manual and half of Jordan High called

Bunchie their leader, in those days. He was the leader of the Black Panthers and an former leader of the Slauson gang. The principal and the police feared him. He was the biggest reason the security at schools began carrying guns.

"WHAT DO WE WANT?" said the black leather clad Bunchie.

"FREEDOM!" said the cheering mob crowding onto San Pedro Street.

"WHEN DO WE WANT IT?"

"NOW!!! FREEDOM, NOW!!!

'Just the memory made him shiver. That urgency made his blood boil even though he had only a vague idea, then, of what he wanted.

'It had been Brother Charles who put flesh on the skinny freedom dream that Bunchie and the Panthers had left on the East Side streets after the riots.

"Freedom," had said the old Muslim, "is having and controlling land. Everything else is a trick."

'Well, it seemed like Bunchie 'nem only wanted some jobs and mortgages on some houses crosstown. They wanted white folks' respect at all the universities. It wound up getting them killed.

(Ray Ray never set foot on a college campus unless you counted the 8 Tray stroll on Saturdays at Pepperdine. He had a problem with white people. He didn't like to do what they told him to do, and they never did what he told them or asked them for that matter.)

'He had seen a movie called "The Spook that Sat by the Door", a long time ago, and he had thought it was a dream or something in his mind for years until the last time he had pulled a bid in the county jail and run across the book by a dude named Charles Greenlee from Chicago. It was all about this old time gangbanger who had become the first black C.I.A. spy, except they wouldn't really let him spy because he was black, so he pulls his bid with the C.I.A. and heads back for Chicago to teach the Cobras (he had always heard them called Egyptian Cobras before that) how to start a revolution. It's like the guy is going to force the government to bargain with him for some control of some of this ground in America.

'That made sense because it was obvious that a lot of the neighborhoods in Watts, on the East Side, and what was now called South Central L.A. were not being controlled very well. He knew he could do as good a job of taking care of the neighborhood as anybody could.

'He would have 5,000 Crips standing behind him when he talked. And, since every gang set in town was proud of Jimmie Black (and almost every Crip set was claiming him as an O.G. member), it would be no problem to get them together to hear Jimmie rap. Just so he said what Ray Ray wanted, and that was unify. Let East and West Side Crips come together. The pie is big enough for everybody, but we must divide it ourselves. No more can we let our common enemies divide and conquer us.'

What was so cool was that Ray Ray knew Jimmie would say exactly that. It was clocked into his genes like almost everybody else who was born and raised in the neighborhood. A lot of the misunderstanding was with people who had come from back East or Down South and were all over L.A. now.

"Ray Ray, what it is, Homeboy?" said Cartoon, spokesman for the small mob of East Coast Crips gathered in the record shop.

"Where's Grip Shot, Cartoon? I need to talk to him about serious business," said Ray Ray, not wanting to parley with the East Coast Crip lieutenant.

"Grip is laid out at the crib on the new drug. You hip to freebase cocaine, yet Ray Ray?"

" Yeh, Cuzz, I'm hip to it, and I'm too hip for it. Tell Grip Shot to call me," said Ray Ray not wanting to tell Cartoon about the big meeting before telling his leader. It would make Grip Shot look bad to come off his high and hear everybody telling him about the big meeting before he knew anything about it. It was the kind of thing that powerful leaders didn't do to each other. And, the meeting was at least a week away. There were still details to be ironed out. The cops hadn't even released Jimmie, yet.

For the first time, Yusuf had mixed emotions about leaving the County Jail. He was ambivalent as he said his, "As Salaamu Alaikum's" to the small group of Muslims that he was leaving. The jail no longer held trepidation for him. He knew the psychology of prison, now, and every man there either loved or respected him -- some begrudgingly, but most loved and respected him highly. It was as if he had made the pro's in sports or was a war hero who had returned home.

But, the streets were full of unknown expectations and complex problems. He knew what Ray Ray would be thinking. Whenever they had spent a rare moment alone, it was all he could talk about -- bringing the East Side and West Side together to control our own neighborhoods, our own destiny.

Yusuf shared the dream with Ray Ray, but though he was a Muslim, he was of little faith. Yet, it was a special prayer of his, too. Now, he was the missing piece in the puzzle. "JIMMIE BLACK" was turning up on the walls in every Crip neighborhood. Of course, he could understand the Hoover 'hoods: 107, 8 Tray HCG, 74's, 59's and 5 Duce, but when Yusuf started to hear that East Coast, Grape Street and even some Bloods were claiming him and bombing buildings with JIMMIE BLACK, it really struck him.

Nobody was crossing his name out either, which was the greatest honor because he hadn't heard of that since the revolution in the late 60's when Melvin X would paint his name and "Revolution NOW" or some other revolutionary saying on walls in every neighborhood in the ghetto. He reflected on how proud he had been when he met Melvin X.

Ray Ray had introduced them. Ray Ray and Melvin X were both from the Fremont area around Florence and Avalon. Yusuf remembered how much he admired the brother and how proud he was when Melvin X had given him the Black Power handshake and the Black Power sign.

He and Ray Ray walked around for days with their chests stuck out. A couple of years after that Melvin X had been killed. Everybody in the neighborhood said the police had assassinated him. It was the first time he remembered feeling morose. It was the way you must have felt when a close relative died.

Ray Ray had quit school and started staying high every day. He wrote "Melvin X (R.I.P.)" all over the neighborhood. Then his mother moved over on Hoover, and he wrote it all over Hoover. Nobody ever crossed out Melvin X but the cops.

Now, Yusuf knew he would see that look in youngsters' eyes when they were introduced to him. It would be deja vu. That would be great, but he had always had a philosophy of staying out of the limelight. Heroes lived well but seemed to die young, probably because of the strife. Anyone who really loved the neighborhood had to continue to fight against the system that kept them powerless.

The time was fast approaching for the people in the community to own and control their destiny, and sometimes frustration and leadership equals violence. When Yusuf mused upon the black men whom he had seen die or knew of who died because they demurred at the wrong time on the wrong spot in the neighborhood, it troubled an emotional kinship in his blood. These were thoughts he consciously avoided, but, he knew Ray Ray concentrated on them everyday.

Still, an even greater dilemma awaited him -- Carole, his big butt problem. She had caused Li'l Jimmie to be put in a foster home, and even though he was sure he could get his son back, what would the boy come back to? A mother and a sister who harangued him for the slightest mistake. He was almost sure Carole did not hate little Jimmie, but she treated him like it. It really differed only in intensity from the beratings that most boys in the neighborhood grew up under, but, now, as a Muslim, could he knowingly allow his boy to be distorted -- emasculated by his mother like most of the boys in Watts?

The release processing was arduous as always, his heart, now, pumping street passion.   His mind was pregnant but apprehensive.

The idea came to him as the police clerk was preparing his final papers before exiting.

"Name?"

"Yusuf Bilal."

The perky little white clerk was perplexed. It didn't compute. There was no Yusuf Bilal being released today, and this guy was black. What kind of name was that for a black? Then, she remembered the staff development on blacks using their Muslim names. The policy was to respectfully request...

"The name you were arrested under, please," she said, hoping the quick smile that punctuated her request would insure the proper communication.

"I was arrested under the name of Jimmie Black, the name my mother gave me in honor of a father I never knew. Unfortunately, it's been more of a curse than an honor for me," he said half seriously.

Jimmie watched the look of recognition creep into her eyes. Suddenly, she became a woman to him. No longer a grey white machine in the system, but a womb and mind.

"Mr. Bla... Bilal. Of course, I have your records. Just a moment, please."

Then, looking up with the kind of sincerity he had only seen in white faces on movie screens and boxed up in television, she stammered, "Mr. Bilal, I would just like to say that all of... most of uh... the ladies and especially those of us who are mothers, greatly admire what you did for your son and his friend... I just want to wish you good luck, and I'm sure everything is going to turn out all right."

It turned out that her name was Sgt. Sanchez (when the woman began to blossom in her, he realized she was a Latina), and the Latino community considered Jimmie Black a hero, too.

It was obvious that if he wanted to keep a low profile, he would have to be two people with two different names and personalities: Jimmie Black, hero, erstwhile killer and community legend, replete with all the delusions and absurd expectations; and, Yusuf Bilal, devout Muslim, father, small businessman, student of Islam, and soon to be college student.

On the one hand, his future was like Ray Ray's, narrow and probably fated for an early death on the South Central streets. But, on the other hand, he could unburden himself of others' expectations.

No longer would people in authority be able to look at him as if he had a glass forehead and tombstones in his eyes. It was a rebirth. Yusuf Bilal -- Yusuf for Joseph, the surrogate father of Esau (Jesus) -- and Bilal for Bilal ibn Rabah, an Islamic pioneer, the first African convert of Prophet Muhammad (S.W.A.S).

Jimmie Black was a name of the past and he would use it to open up the best of the past, but Yusuf Bilal was his name for the future, and he would use it to open up the bright, shiny world that he planned for the future.

Chapter 12
Ray Ray's Dream

Ray Ray was working and planning fast and furiously. The time seemed just right. Old Crips were getting tired of gang warring and being poor, while most of the youngsters didn't really know what they were fighting each other for -- not that it kept them from dipping their fingers in blood, almost daily.

He was down with the oldheads in all the East Coast and Hoover sets, and his contacts in 107 Hoover would pull Grape Street and all the Watts Crips. The biggest problem was going to be getting the West Side. The oldest west side gang, Rollin' 30's (Harlem Crips) was cool and would be down for Consolidated Crip, but Eight Tray Gangsters and Rollin' 60's were mavericks.

They were historically, the same bloodline-- spoiled, wild, west side pioneers, athletes and killers. ETG was probably the biggest single black gang in L.A. Their neighborhood was serene, middleclass, and high rent except for the ETG and 8 Tray Gangster signs that had taken over all the wall space: store fronts, elementary/ junior high and high schools, and parks from Crenshaw to Vermont and Florence to Manchester.

Trays had even taken over Pepperdine University on 79th and Vermont by forcing them to move. In fact, that was why Ray Ray planned to have the big meeting on the sprawling abandonded campus of Pepperdine where the 8 Trays often met on Sunday.

Their leader was a youngster called Mobster who almost filled up a room by himself. He was still a teenager, but driving iron and other jail conditioning had given him the look of a pro linebacker-- huge, rippling arms, big chest, tapering into a small waist and hips. Mobster was uncharacteristically no dummy, however. His initiation of the Tray van had taken gang war to a level of refined terrorism.

But, for all their fiendishness, even the 8 Trays were tame compared to the Rolling 60's. The 60's and Trays had been down (close) with each other until, recently, but, now, the rumor was that they were about to tear into each other because of a misunderstanding about their 'Lettes (women).

Ray Ray figured it had more to do with territory because 60's were growing faster than any gang in gang history. Horace Mann Junior High was pumping out more 60's than graduates, and Crenshaw High was raw for anybody who wasn't at least an undercover Sixty. The Avenues were havens for them, and if someone was unlucky enough to trespass upon 60's turf and get caught in a nest of them smoking reefer and drinking Olde English 800 malt liquor, they killed without human compassion.

They were expanding in almost every direction. They were laying claim to all the unclaimed territory on the west side of Crenshaw, and they had a tenuous coalition with Rollin' 30's on the north, but open warfare between Eight Trays and 60's was about to break out on their eastern (Western Avenue) and southern (Florence Avenue) boundaries.

The Rollin' 60's were passionate wall writers, leaving no business, school, park, block wall around a home or even church unchristened with "Rollin' 60 Crips" or "R.S.C." Now, they were hitting up walls in Tray hood.

What puzzled Ray Ray the most about the Rollin' 60's was that they really had no leader, and sometimes 60's would kill 60's and mutilate their victims' bodies. The police were even rumored to be afraid of them because many of them were so young that life meant nothing. What each individual Rollin' 60 wanted more than anything else was a reputation among the other Rollin' 60's.

Yes, Rollin' 60 Crip and 8 Tray Gangster Crip were the only two missing pieces remaining in Ray Ray's dream of bringing 5,000 Crips together at Pepperdine to talk about consolidating under one secret leadership.

Chapter 13
Crip's His Daddy

After Ray Ray explained his plan to capture large parts of Los Angeles for "The Neighborhood" as he termed it, Yusuf had to admit the plan sounded plausible.

"But, Ray Ray, I just don't want to go down on wrong's side. It's too weak. If I commit to you, I could die for nothing, but if I commit to Allah and brothers at the masjid, I'll at least be secure that my dying will be for a righteous cause.

"This is deeper than dope, cocaine. When the cocaine supply shifts, y'all may go back to robbing liquor stores to keep up the cash flow. I can't deal with that. I want something bigger than that. I want t h e i r minds, not just a name, not their fear. I want to put some things on their minds from now through the 21st Century.

"Yeh, I'll talk. I'll talk about unity, but I'm going to have to teach some Islam, too."

It stunned Ray Ray. He knew Jimmie was a Muslim, but it wasn't everyday that somebody told him no. He recoiled and hit Jimmie with a reality that was undeniable.

"Your boy's a Crip, Jimmie..."

"It's Yusuf."

"Yeh, well, Yusuf, your youngster is J-Mack from 2 or 3 different sets, and the County is his momma, now, so Crip's his daddy, and I AM Crip.

When you'll feel lucky to see him once or twice in a year -- and I heard the courts won't let you or your wife see him at all for a couple years -- I'll have him everyday cause he's Crippin'.

"Now, you talk to these youngsters, and you tell 'em what I want you to say... ," Ray Ray seethed.

The motel room was air conditioned against the abnormally hot Spring day. It was in one of several that Ray Ray was rumored to have bought since he had become "nouveau riche" in the cocaine trade. It had been airy and pleasant until, now.

It was perfect -- Ray Ray and him, some Golden Bird chicken. It was like the old days when they would come together in similar tete-a-tete's and swear to take over. And, again, Ray Ray was trying to push him into something, disrespect him. It had happened before, but no more.

"Ray Ray, you and I will be tearing up this room in a minute," said Jimmie, hot blood flushing his face. Then he cooled, mind whirring.

"Look, brother, I come in peace. You don't need me. You know what you want said. Say it. Practice it. Then, when you get it exactly like you want it, say it. Tell 'em that I had to go to the mosque, but I'm with them in spirit. As Salaamu Alaikum."

Yusuf slammed the door of the motel room, Ray Ray's words still ringing in his ears.

'Your son is J-Mack from 2 or 3 different sets ... Crip is his daddy... the courts won't let you or your wife see him at all for a couple years... a couple years...'

Chapter 14
Ray Ray's Big Meeting

"We are one. Eastside and Westside Crips... even Bloods. There will be no turning to the police to settle our battles." Ray Ray talked slowly, confidently, relishing the sight of 5,000 Crips sitting and standing on the lawn of Pepperdine University. The Trays had supplied a makeshift stand and portable mike.

"We will fight because we are fighters -- Crip means fighter, but we are fighting to be winners, successful. We are fighting to control the neighborhoods. It will happen... many murders from now.

"But, let me explain to you what is happening because I might not live to see 5,000 Crips come together, again. There is an organization being built in

South Central L.A. It came out of the Watts riots when gangsters went underground and became Panthers, Muslims, and the US Organization. It came to us as Crip in 1971 before most of y'all got out of grade school.

"There's going to be a drug war in the neighborhoods. It's going to involve us because we are the killers. Just like Capone in the 20's formed a crime organization we know and respect as the Mafia, an organization of that nature is being formed right here.

"Remember, we are one-- Eastside, Westside Crips, even Bloods. There will be no turning to the police to settle our battles. And you don't have to do wrong all the time to get over. When you get money, buy some property, business or something."

Suddenly Bear rushed up to Ray Ray and pushed a note into his hand roughly. It broke his rhythm.

"I, I..." the crowd started getting progressively noisy.

"TRAYS AND 60'S ARE PACKING AND THERES GONNA BE A SHOOTOUT EITHER HERE OR SOMEWHERE TONITE," it read.

The rumor spread quickly, but everybody had felt that it might go down sooner or later. Ray Ray knew he wasn't going to be able to say what he had planned. He decided to snatch bits of what he had so carefully prepared.

"You are greater than that. Listen to where it is really at.

Calling all Crips. Calling all Crips. Come in Crips. Come in Crips.

Come in Breakin' Poplockin' Crips.
The time for Crip gangs is dead.
It's time for Crip organization instead."

Then Ray Ray started throwing up gang signs. He started by flying the Crip "C" with his thumb and forefinger. Then he flashed 107, 8-Tray Hoover, 59, 74, and 5 Duce. His hands moved smoothly from one of the deadly signals to a flurry of others: 8-Tray, 90, Rollin' 60, Rollin' 30.

The crowds of youths sectored off on the lush green lawn sent an orgasm of cheering rising through the abandoned campus as Ray Ray Crip danced. Now, he was throwing up Blood signs: VNG's Swans and 20's.

Everybody just kind of split to their hoods. Deadly enemies crossed paths with hardly a look. The air was thick with danger as devoted killers made their ways back to the neighborhoods.

Chapter 15
Jimmie Jr. Makes a Friend

"**Y**o daddy is Fass Jimmie Black, O.G. Crip to the max."

"Huh?" said Little Jimmie, instantly knowing he was wrong, slow again. He had to think faster, now, all the Crips in town were treating him like gold or something fine. It was like the whole city had his back after that week the L.A. Sentinel printed his father's picture and a big story about the night when Allah had made him into an angel to save Flaco and himself in the alley. He felt he must do things differently, better.

He had tried to remember everything his father had ever said to him, the hard teachings that had come before the beatings, the whispered street teachings at corners on Manchester and Main or Broadway and Florence. He remembered, though it never quite came out right when he tried to explain it to Termite, who he was running with again.

"Look, Slick Jimmie, you can Crip Walk on Main Street past the 77th Street Police Station in broad daylight or night. You got the top spot, Cuzz," teased Termite.

"We got to take big chances, Cuzz. We got to do big things. We got to live up to yo' reputation in the neighborhood, Cuzz."

Jimmie had stayed in 3 different foster homes and 2 different neighborhoods since then. Nothing had turned out like he thought it would, except he learned how to be more cunning on the streets.

He had learned to not focus on being unable to see his daddy and transferred that love to his homies: Termite, Cartoon, Ken Dog, Li'l V-Dog, the whole Hoover Set -- 5 Duce, 5 Nine, 74's, 8 Tray Hoover, and 107 O.G.'s. Because of his father's fame and having to move so much, Jimmie knew Crips on every set. He even knew a few 60's and East Coases that he liked.

Jimmie was, now, thirteen, and puberty was his biggest concern. It controlled his body totally at times. He was constantly stimulated and most of the time sexually. It constantly distracted him. Termite understood perfectly because he was caught up in it, too.

Jimmie somehow knew it was wrong to "do it", and it confused, then, perplexed him. The one lesson that he remembered best was the one his daddy taught over and over again.

"Don't put your semen inside a woman, Li'l Jimmie, unless you love her, and if you love her, marry her. Fornication is the sign of weakness, lack of discipline. Muslims avoid it. It's a great sin."

Every time they passed a prostitute switching and twitching down Main Street, he would say it again. It was no problem for him, then. He had been 9, but since he had been taken away from his daddy and started living on the Westside, it was becoming difficult. Being a Westside Crip was mostly having sex or trying to have sex with your lady or some new lady.

Lady Tee, who called herself his lady, would pull him down on beds, then pull his shorts down. The first time she did it he pulled away, but she was 16, and her hippy frame was too heavy to push off.

"You gon' give it up, today, Li'l Jimmie. I'm gon' bust your cherry, today," she giggled.

His intuition told him that she almost thought she could force him even if he didn't let her, but they had been boxing, just fooling around. He had slapped her hard, and she fell, but as she pulled herself up around his legs they began wrestling.

"You know you wanna do it," she said.

How could he lie? He was hard as Superman's Elbow...

"Batman's Kneecap..." said Termite.

"Hard as old folk's toenails," laughed Jimmie, and they fell out and gave each other some dap. Jimmie could never get past this point in retelling the incident.

Having sex with Lady Tee had gotten him instant respect among his homies. The girls stopped smarting off at him, and his homeboys stopped treating him young.

Lady Tee bragged about him when he was around and when he was not. She never told anybody that he wouldn't come in her.

"You rocking the cradle in your snatch, girl. Yo' li'l boyfriend is in the 7th grade," bagged Charmayne, as she and Lady Tee crossed Florence headed toward Horace Mann Junior High.

"He's in the 8th, Ho, and what's up! So what. This our third year in 8th grade. He gone graduate cause he's smart. What's up?" Lady Tee replied in strictly Crip jargon that always challenged the person talked to whether serious or in jest.

"You love him. Don' cha, girl?" said Charmayne.

"Love his dirty drawers. Sometimes I be sittin' up in class just thinking about him and my pants get wet. I wanna have his baby. I'm tired of school. I'm Special Ed, and I ain't never gonna graduate. I shoulda been done had a baby."

"He don't love you, Talesha. He don't love nothin' but Crippin'."

"I don't care. I love him enough for both of us, and I wouldn't even like him it he wasn't a Crip. I was born a Crip, and so was he. He understands me, and I understand him. Jimmie gon' be something though, Charmayne. I can tell. Jimmie's gonna be famous. I'm just enjoying what I got while I got it. And, when he quits me, it don't matter cause I'm just gonna keep on goin' with him."

In fact, she only went to school to bomb his name on Horace Mann's walls, desks, and books.

"O.G. Jimmie Mack" or "J-Mack, O.G. Killer".

Rollin' 60's and 8 Trays claimed Li'l Jimmie because Mann was a 60's school, and though Jimmie was down with Hollister, Jay Stone and all the O.G. 60's at school, he lived on 70th and Budlong in the Tray hood. Termite was 8 Tray Hoover and introduced him to all the 8 Tray Gangsters that he knew in Jimmie's neighborhood, but when some E.T.G's or R.S.C's asked him what set he was from, he would proudly say, "107 O.G. Hoover Crip Gangsters."

He had a few minor scuffles in the bathroom on the third floor at first, but since the word got around about who he was, he didn't even have that problem. His real problem was that his little head was telling his big head what to do, and Lady Tee knew it.

She was always starting some stuff with somebody and he would often have to bust up some mark who had slapped her or punched her.

It was cool, at first. She would just point the dude out, and if he was about the same size, Jimmie would come up beside him and steal to the jaw. If he was too big, Jimmie would ditch 6th period and wait for him outside with his iron pole. One good lick was enough for even the biggest 8th grader.

But, now, Jimmie felt that he couldn't lose a fight. His reputation was so big and meant so much to him that he couldn't stand the embarrassment. He even stopped boxing because he couldn't take anybody getting the best of him. It didn't matter to him if they were older or bigger.

"Jimmie come up to school with me tomorrow," Lady Tee pleaded.

"They be playing too much up there, Tee. I laugh and I joke and I drink a lotta cokes, but I don't play no more. I be done killed one of them marks up there foolin' with me." Jimmie meant it, too. He was getting mean and he liked it.

Lady Tee's face lit up. Her thick lips turned up in a leering, lascivious smile.

"Would you kill somebody for me, Jimmie?" she prodded. Then, she wanted to have sex. Jimmie played her off real cold, but he had to lie and say he couldn't because he was going over to the East Side to try to find his old man.

He found himself sitting on the bus stop on Manchester as if not able to turn the lie loose. He had really wanted to go to the East Side and try to ask around for his daddy, but he didn't want to see his momma, and the East Side was still kind of scary when you were by yourself.

He thought about walking through the 8 Tray park (St. Andrews at Manchester), but the Tray park was hot with busters this time of year (October, still early in the school year).

"Do you know if this bus goes to Central or not, Jim?" said the clipped accent dressed in gray Member's Only jacket and skinny tie.

Then came the questions. "Wasn't he in Mrs, Cavil's homeroom? Didn't he run track? Why wasn't he coming to school, lately?"

"What are you, the police or something?" managed Jimmie, but somehow he felt glad to be talking to Weldon whom he recognized as one of the kids who seemed to think they owned Horace Mann. He was student council something or other, and his girl friend was Quintana, the finest 13 year old Jimmie had ever seen.

Not used to having conversations with boys like Weldon, Jimmie didn't know quite what to say next. He found himself saying almost apologetically, "I'm in Quintana's homeroom. She f-fine man."

Weldon taken a little aback by the bold admission, said, "She's smart, too."

"You gettin' that?" Jimmie laughingly asked and playfully shot a jab to Weldon's somewhat beefy ribcage.

"Well, almost..." said Weldon, forsaking his oath and religious vows to never tell, for the delight of total communication with a respected peer.

"Next time I go over to her house and her mother leaves us alone downstairs in her great big basement, I think I'll get her cause last time I had her bra..."

"Don't go for the bra, man. Go for the gold," said Jimmie, feeling "too" slick and experienced.

The bus came and Weldon and Jimmie sat in the seats right behind the driver. (Jimmie usually sat in the back.) Every time the bus stopped to let on some new passengers, there would be at least one person who knew Weldon, and by the time they reached Broadway there were about 8 of them sitting in the front of the bus brazenly discussing sex. They were having such a good time talking that Jimmie decided to just keep riding. When they reached Central Avenue and Weldon got off, Jimmie got off with him.

"I'm gonna be truthful, Jim, I never have actually done it to a girl," confessed Weldon, "but I think I know how."

"You don't have to be scared, Well - Done. Some girls don't care if you know how to or not," said Jimmie.

"I would like to, but the only person I ever tried to with is Quintana, and she wants to wait until we get married -- June 19th, 1986."

"You crazy Well- Done, but you my homeboy. I know somebody you can do it to right now."

Weldon could tell that Jimmie was serious. His hormones were crying out.

"Let's get back on the Manchester bus, and go back to the Hood. I know a broad who will give you all you want if I tell her to."

Weldon was immediately aroused with the notion. Just to see a girl naked and maybe touch her there. The thought made him throb. He started acting real silly.

"You mean, right now, today, in a few skinny minutes?" He laughed and stuck out his palm. "Give me five," said Weldon in his slickest tone.

"Straight like that, Cuzz," said Jimmie, giving him some dap as they crossed the street to catch the bus.

Weldon's mind raced. 'Was he going to be in danger? Jimmie was a Crip. Everybody knew that. Is that what Crips did when they stayed out of school? To get "all he wanted" whenever he wanted. It seemed unbelievable. But, what about protection, a prophylactic. He wasn't sure how to use one if he had one.' The bus sped across Vermont thru 4:00 P.M. traffic.

"Maybe we better stop and get some protection, Cuzz," said Weldon.

"You don't have to worry about it. She take care of everything," said Jimmie reflecting on how Lady Tee would always douche immediately afterwards, until recently.

By the time they got to Western and began the 3 block walk north to Tee's house, Weldon had almost ejaculated.

"I hope her parents aren't home."

"She ain't got no parents, just a momma, and she ain't never home. She got a little brother, but he's my little homeboy."

They turned west on 85th toward a graffiti spattered fourplex. "E.T.G" was bombed on the door of the first floor apartment. Jimmie disdained the front door, hearing the droning rap record "Rapper's Delight..." coming from the alley entrance, he pushed through the door directly into the bedroom of the one bedroom apartment.

Lady Tee was stretched out on the bed in some tight Jordache jeans, and she started to smile, seeing Jimmie, but her face changed when she saw Weldon.

"Tee, this my homeboy, Well Done."

"I know Weldon Brown. He ain't no Crip."

"Yeh, but he cool, Tee. Let me rap to you," and Jimmie took her in the kitchen.

"Say, baby, I want you to do me a favor and turn my partner on to a piece."

Tee had been rubbing herself against the pillow underneath her mother's soft velour spread when they arrived. She laughed and unzipped the Jordaches. By the time she returned to the tiny pink walled bedroom, the jeans had begun to slide down revealing her drawerless hips and thighs.

Weldon had taken a seat in the corner next to the door, and the sight of her sauntering naked indifference sent his blood gushing to every appendage of his body.

This girl whom he barely had met sat perched on the bed naked from the bottom down waiting to have sex with him. His body was no longer his own. His legs sent him hurtling toward her. His lips reached lustily for her lips, his hand for her...

"No, no kissing. Kissing is when you love somebody. I don't love nobody but Jimmie!"

The rejection shook Weldon to his senses. "You... you're Jimmie's girl?"

The emotion began to ebb in him. He had never considered this was Jimmie's girl, like Quintana was his girl. He had said "a broad." The term connoted tramp or community property. How could he do this to his new friend's girl? Would Jimmie expect to have sex with Quintana? Probably not, but this was wrong.

"I didn't know. I don't wanna with my friend's gir... lady. That's not my style."

Lady Tee suddenly felt shamefully naked. She pulled the velour spread around herself and gave Weldon her most contemptuous look.

"Jimmie, come get this mark out of here. I thought you and me were going to do it. We can't do nothing with no mark around," but her tone belied her shame.

"Get him out of here," she screamed, beginning to cry.

It impressed Jimmie that Weldon could see Tee's naked behind and not have sex with her. How many times he, himself, had daydreamed about the sight of it. The vision of it was its power. The hidden treat that fourteen year old boys dreamed of, willfully or unwillfully. It bedeviled them. And, here was somebody who turned it down. He had to know something.

Weldon was homey -- super straight most times. But, he was filled out and good size. If it wasn't for that square, too friendly smile of his. He smiled at everybody -- people without knowing them, drunks, drug addicts, old ladies, and almost all young ladies. Sometimes Jimmie had him figured for scared, but he wasn't. He was just friendly.

"Let's shoot some ball."

"Where?" said Jimmie, his mind racing for something else to do. He didn't see what the big ritual was about ball. It seemed young and always got too rough. He didn't want to fight, and couldn't take losing. It just made him want to fight or play more.

What was the big deal. So, Marques Johnson came out of Crenshaw and was, now, one of the premier forwards in the N.B.A. making millions. That took too long. He could...

"We got the winners," said Weldon who was wearing Adidas and suddenly started bouncing around and looking like he wanted the ball.

They warmed up and waited their turn on Horace Mann's courts out by the gymnasium that was rumored to be opened in 15 minutes. They were playing full court, and you didn't dare get too acrobatic on the Horace Mann asphalt.

Jimmie felt so comfortable when he finally got to the courts, but the school itself had become ominous for him. He wouldn't go during school hours for fear of running into his homeroom teacher, or one of the deans who harassed him. But, after school, Mann was the Rollin' 60's hangout, and there didn't seem to be anything more exhilarating than being on the Crip set.

Now, however, the music was blasting from 3 different parts of the playground -- two tapes of George Clinton's "Atomic Dog" and the radio station starting arguments. It seemed like everybody was up in each other's face trying to start something, calling each other out. Li'l gangsters challenging bigger gangsters and friends jumping in. Every now and then a skirmish would break out, but it would be some "wanna be's" trying to find each other out, nothing serious.

Jimmie and a few other O.G.'s and their friends who crowded the center court were immune from the feel me out hassles that the 60's played in little packs of six and eight around the expansive grounds. They were respected as killers -- deserved their due. There were ample stories of wanna be's who had prematurely hassled an O.G. and become an instant mark for a murder.

Jimmie knew that before something went down it would have to come through all the wanna be's first, and by the time he saw them scattering he knew where the 60's had a gun hidden in a dumpster, or he could take about 20 different ways out of there.

All of a sudden the playground chatter went up two levels. The ripple of noise started coming toward center court where Weldon and Jimmie were waiting their game.

"It's Hollister," said Weldon, obviously elated at the thought of playing with the best at Horace Mann.

The game stopped. The players came over to congratulate Hollister and Ken Bone for beating John Muir Junior High and keeping Mann undefeated.

The two talented youngsters moved with the grace and confidence of champions. They wore purple Lakers' jackets and some sneakers that had the whole playground pointing, admiringly.

"I love it," said Weldon, tiptoeing and high fiving Hollister.

"Come to class sometime, why don' cha? Miss Spinzer is pissed. You're gonna get a "D".

Hollister was caught up in the applause and sizing up the crowd for players. He was arrogant, but everybody seemed to love him and understand. He was the latest phenom. Destined for greatness in hoop history -- a can't miss. A gifted student in the classroom and in the gym. It was a given that he would follow in the U.C.L.A. tradition that had begun to filter down from Crenshaw High School via Marques Johnson.

But, lately the star had begun to dim. Hollister had started skipping school (except fordays when the basketball team played) and preferred to play on his fiberglass backboard with Ken Bone and the 60's behind his house on 7th Avenue all day.

"Strawberry just left," said Weldon. He says he's tired of waitin' around to play you," laughed Weldon.

"I missed him, again!" Hollister cursed, anxious for the inevitable confrontation with his idol: Strawberry, 6'4", 200 pounds who had just graduated from Mann and was immediately making a name for himself at Crenshaw.

"Let's run some full court, Weldon. I can get the gym opened," said Hollister.

"You want to play Mr. Micken's homeroom. They won the homeroom championship," Weldon offered, always sweetening the pot.

They had to argue with the janitor, Mr. Smith to get Ken Bone in because everybody knew Bone was a Crip and subject to go crazy at any time.

"I'll be cool, Mr. Smith. I'm sorry bout the walls and stuff, but that's Crazy Freddy. I got your back, Cuzz. Lemme play," pried Ken Bone.

Smith relented, remembering how much he had begged to get into gyms in Watts during the 50's.

It was obvious from the opening tip that Homeroom 205 was overmatched. They were organized at first, but Hollister and Ken Bone were too good a tandem. They seemed to move on rollerskates while the others' sneakers were nailed to the floor. It was embarrassing. Jimmie saw that he couldn't keep up so he started hanging in the backcourt on the fast breaks (which were frequent) and playing defense. Once he took the ball out after a score and hit Ken Bone with a pass about 3/4 of the court away. Bone streaked to the goal and dunked on his third step for the win.

"30-12, Fool!" Jimmie heard himself almost scream. He had never felt this good playing before.

There were only 3 teams with gumption enough to come inside the gym, and the combination of Weldon, Jimmie, Hollister, Ken Bone, and Jimmie Trice was running the others' tongues out.

They relinquished the court gladly after winning four straight -- two against the homeroom champs who had been reduced to the ranks of Hollister and Ken Bone's sycophants.

"I feel so good, Cuzz. I could kill somebody," said Hollister. They slapped hands and laughed before the ridiculousness of the statement could take hold.

Weldon started talking real fast in another direction, but the tone of the conversation had been set.

"You think you could, Cuzz? You think you could really kill a fool?" probed Ken Bone. "I don't know if I could, yet, Cuzz. Let's kill somebody, tonight."

"Tonight? Naw, Fool. If I kill somebody, it's gonna be planned, you know, thought out, so I don't get caught, Cuzz. You probably won't even know about it, Cuzz, cause you talk too much," Hollister bagged on his homeboy and laughed. Everybody slapped Hollister's hand.

"I got a strap (gun)," Jimmie heard himself saying coolly like he had heard it rapped on the East Side, "and, I'm itching to kill somebody white."

"Naw, Cuzz. You going to jail for a million years, Cuzz. You better kill one of these poot butts around here, Cuzz, so the police won't be looking for you that hard. You crazy, Jimmie. I seen how you looked at the principal in the office that day, Cuzz. You really don't like that white man, huh?"

"You's a killer, Slick Jimmie. Anybody can see it in your eyes," said Hollister admiringly.

"Why don't you claim Rollin' 60, Jimmie? We can take out a chump this summer. We can rule Crenshaw High next year. We can sew up the women, the dope, the basketball, the women, everything, Cuzz," said Ken Bone, unaware that he had said women twice, moving to his feet and standing over Jimmie, almost preaching.

"You better try to just make it through the summer, Cuzz. Between that water (PCP) and them I.F.B.'s (Inglewood Family Bloods) you might not see September, Cuzz."

Jimmie came down on Ken Bone so hard that Bone had to throw a punch, but Jimmie could tell by the look in his face that there was no malice or threat in the blow. Ken Bone was better than him at basketball, but boxing was another thing.

They scuffled a little and started to draw a crowd. Jimmie shot two harmless jabs at Ken Bone and moved inside, butting him underneath the chin with his head, laughing as the blood oozed out of Bone's lip.

"Why you do that, Cuzz? You always doing something dirty." Ken Bone was angry at the taste of his blood. His tongue was probing the cut inside the bottom of his lip. He started to go crazy, but Jimmie had handled him too easily. He was too bloodthirsty. So, Ken Bone played it off.

"Let's go run some ball at the 'Shaw," Hollister said grabbing their Laker jackets and coming between Ken Bone and Jimmie.

Weldon and Jimmie seemed to be together, so Hollister withheld expanding his invitation. Weldon's game was soft. Jimmie Black was kind of crude but tough and daring, a winner.

"Jimmie Black, why don't you come play with us when we play Carver, next week?" offered Hollister, leaving without waiting for a response.

The crowd went back to the game with more ammunition for the sport of legend making that was played in the bathrooms, nooks, and crannies of Horace Mann, easily the most infamous junior high school in Los Angeles, possibly in the world.

Nobody could talk like Mann kids. Nobody could play basketball, football, fight, curse or kill as well as this hybridization of new middle class spoiled brats from the bungalows in the Avenues and East Side, first generation, abject-poverty-free, apartment dwellers.

By homeroom tomorrow the amplified eyewitness accounts of the basketball games and the quick skirmish between would-be killers would be one more reason for the mere mortal kids at Mann to cultivate anecdotes about their celebrated peers. Just being around them was being a part of history in the making.

Chapter 16
The Beginning of a New Life

Jimmie was surprised when Weldon asked him to come home with him for dinner. Nobody but Flaco had ever asked him that before. He had been over to lots of his friends' houses, but usually while their mothers were gone, and if they ate, it was like stealing from the refrigerator.

When they reached the beautiful white bungalow on West Blvd., Jimmie was not surprised to see the new Cadillac Seville parked in the driveway, but the sight of Weldon's dad made him nervous. He wanted to remember his manners because these were respectable people, and he wanted them to like him.

After he was introduced to Weldon's mom, dad, and two younger brothers, they sat down to eat dinner. The table was long and mahogany brown to match the chairs and plush brown carpet.

Jimmie couldn't recall being in a house quite so elegant. He washed his hands in the best smelling bathroom that he had ever been in, but he couldn't bring himself to dirty the perfect set of pink guest towels, so he dried his hands with toilet tissue and flushed it afterwards.

Weldon's father didn't look much like him except around the eyes and mouth. Weldon was tallish, tan and almost plump, but his father was shorter, dark and thin. He spoke with a confident tone and firm stare. It was like you were being read. Jimmie noticed that it made Weldon and his brothers almost as nervous to have their father, Mr. Brown, talk to them as it did himself. Weldon's dad spoke openly about hidden things.

"You better start using deodorant everyday after you shower, Weldon. You stinking up the whole table, Son." This made everyone laugh. Mrs. Brown even had to hold back a snicker.

"When you turn 13 and go through puberty, you start to grow hair under your arms and sweat," Mr. Brown continued.

The realization struck Jimmie dumbfounded.

"You're going to have to bathe everyday. Don't miss a day, and shower after you play at school, too. You need it if you still think you're a ladies' man," Mr. Brown taunted.

Jimmie suddenly realized how much he missed and needed his daddy. Tears rushed to his eyes, and he had to play it off like he was going to the bathroom, again. When he finally found the pink, fluffy toilet and sink in what he was sure had to be a mansion, it occurred to him that he might stink. He didn't use deodorant, and there was never anyone counting the baths he took. He tried to shower when he thought about it, but he didn't like to bathe without changing clothes, and he washed his own clothes, lately, so that just didn't happen much.

He probably did stink sometimes. Maybe even now. It made him feel uneasy and strange. He tried to smell underneath his arms, but he couldn't tell. One thing was certain. The bathroom smelled great. He probably did smell bad compared to it.

Jimmie spotted some Brut cologne behind the sink. Something told him that cologne and funk just equaled double funk, so he decided to wipe his T-shirt underneath his arms first. It made a big, wet spot, and he could smell himself as he screwed the bottle of Brut closed and placed it back approximately where it was.

Jimmie decided he was going to leave without telling Weldon and his family. He wasn't sure if he knew his way out, however, so he unhooked the bathroom screen and climbed out of the window into the dark.

The block wall was smooth and about six feet high on that side tapering to a four foot front mounted with wrought iron and a wrought iron gate. He ran his hand across the smooth wall, and his right hand groped in his jeans for his black marker, but...no! If Weldon wouldn't even take off Tee with his permission, he couldn't bomb his pad.

Yet, this was a 'hood that he had never been in before. He had to hit it up. He finally decided on the corner store. "O.G. J-Mack." Look at it... layin' there!

Jimmie didn't have time to admire his handiwork like he would have liked to, but it was that initial exhilaration that always made it so worthwhile. He knew someone would eventually come and cross his art out with their own. He just hoped they were good, and not one of those wanna be's trying to get something started cause they liked to see people die.

The police car slithered past, and a halting voice said, "Hey, you little gangster. G-Get your a-- uh, on home, ya pissy bastard."

Jimmie almost laughed aloud at the white lady policeman leaning out of the black and white cop cruiser. If she really had him made for a gangster or had seen him write his name on the wall, she would have had her partner swoop down on him. The black and white was cruising slowly down West Boulevard headed north, and Jimmie had passed it on the East side of the street headed south. Six paces after they passed each other Jimmie knew there was no way the cops could have caught him.

"No, you're mistaken. Everybody ain't doin' it. Some people are right there but laying back -- all up in the corners not doin' it, this time. Finding slick reasons for why not," said Weldon. He was trying to graduate from junior high.

"I mean it's all about grad nite and graduation. Baddest in the nation, Horace Mann Graduation. I'm Gonna be the sensation, tuxedo situation, controlled vibration. Come join the celebration, just a little concentration for mind domination. The crown of creation. Forget high school -- just a way station -- I'm through with masturbation. I'm ready for procreation.

"I'm down for making a baby, Jim, that I keep. Me and Quintana are too hot for each other to keep from making a baby soon. I just hope I can finish high school, first."

Florence was alive with kids converging at the corner of Western, unloading busses, coming from four different directions. It was the best part of the morning for the bus drivers wiping furrowed brows and waving congratulatorily at each other at having made it through the toughest part of the morning.

Everyone was centered about the hamburger stand which was the nexus for a rumor mill: somebody had a strap; there were some new 8-Trays checking into Mann (shootout after school); two seventh graders had gotten into a fight and one got stabbed; Lamont had won $200 (everybody's money) in the crap game behind the laundromat; Cody had developed a fabulous, unbelievable, poplock move called the one arm tick; Mr. Bilal had gotten off the Florence bus.

Everybody's conversation changed in the Golden Ox. The gratuitous profanity disappeared. The most belligerent wanna be's tried to find recognition in his eyes. "You don't <u>even</u> want to make Mr. Bilal mad, Cuzz."

The 7th graders thought Mr. Bilal used to be a Crip, but the 8th graders knew he was too old for that. He was just unusual because he was a teacher, and he rode the bus, would fight, but didn't cuss, didn't hate Crips, and didn't like the white principal or the police.

Mr. Bilal taught English and everybody wanted to be in his class because it was "live". He played records and tapes between classes and made videotapes of poplockers and poets. He would work you to death, though. But, his classes were loud and active. He had the best (most organized) homeroom basketball team and the best public speakers.

He had gone to bat for gangbangers against other teachers, and the principal hated him. All the kids respected Mr. Bilal more than the principal (whom they didn't even know because they hardly saw him). Mr. Bilal seemed to be everywhere -- on the school ground at lunch, in the bathrooms, at the dances, supervising assemblies, breaking up gang fights, in the dean's office, on the bus, and he knew everybody in the school and everybody who had gone to Horace Mann recently. He commanded respect from the 8-Trays and Rollin' 60's. Secretly, he was called O.G. Bilal.

Jimmie had never heard Mr. Bilal rap. He had heard about him, but he so seldomly darkened the doors of Horace Mann that he had never had a serious run in with the schools most popular teacher. As Mr. Bilal came in the front door of the Golden Ox, Weldon was the first to run up to him and give him a fast five.

"We're doing a black history month assembly at 74th Street Elementary and out in the Valley this week, Weldon. You're doing 'Notes on Commercial Theater', ... 'Same in Blues', ... 'Jungle Man', and two of your own poems. You may have to do the 'I Have a Dream' speech for one assembly at 74th Street, too, so be ready."

"What about another one of my own poems, Mr. Bilal? I got 'Gangbangers' down pat," pleaded Weldon.

"We'll hold it for the anti-gang assembly at the end of the month at Mann," Bilal shot back, forgetting the principal's reluctance to allow his Speech Choir to do another assembly.

Walking in the Golden Ox like this reminded him of McGarry's across from Fremont High in 1965. "Viva La Village" was the greeting in those days. Now, it was "What's up, Cuzz?" Everybody wanting to be a gangster or admiring the gangsters for living the life of defiance. Living their lives in seconds -- heavy drama everyday. Either from the police (the enemy), Trays (deadly misunderstanding), Bloods (blood feud), or one of your own homeboys (your brother).

It had been the same at Fremont in "65" when the Slausons held check, but the Gladiators, Huns, and even the Businessmen (at times) were potential hassles, and your own homey would sweat you in those days, too.

But, Jack Bilal had grown up on these very streets with those same values, and they had never really changed because nothing had happened to justify their changing. He still wanted the same thing these young brothers wanted. He wanted to rule, to be powerful, to control something, anything... a woman, a street corner, then a block, a park, a neighborhood. He knew why the hardcore ones would not go to school. It was another hassle with authority about power (often a physical threat).

His walk relaxed them. It was well oiled. This was the jungle side of Los Angeles and Bilal felt comfortable, respected -- no further need to be tested. But, in 15 minutes when he aimed his squared shoulders through the main office at Horace Mann Junior High School, he would be all nervous energy exploding successfully encountered tests of his skill, integrity, virtue, intestinal fortitude, ph, and religion. The onslaught would be relentless, and his merit at this point in time (being both male and black) was not to be soon established with the school system.

'So, this was the kid everybody was talking about, lately, Jimmie Black,' thought Bilal, as he detected a subtle familiarity about the eyes and mouth. The youngster moved with gifted smoothness. His speech was not profuse but accurate and that clipped, creative, South Central L.A. dialect that engendered instant respect on the streets. There was a humility tempered with aloofness that indicated strong breeding.

Then it struck him. This was little light-in-the-pants Jimmie Black's son. Big Jimmie had been on the front pages so often a few years ago that his ill fitting nickname (forced on him by jealous but older Slausons) seemed even more preposterous.

Bilal had often told the story of the twelve year old kid who had come with the bloods in Slauson Village that night in August, 1965 when every gang in South Central L.A. headed by the Slausons from Fremont to Manual Arts joined up with the Businessmen from South Park, the Huns and the Orientals out of Watts, the Gladiators from the West Side, etc., and declared war against the police for beating up Marquette Frye and his momma in Watts.

The ten year old Jimmie had followed them on their burning sprees as they destroyed Avalon and Broadway. Once the gasoline had leaped from the Clorox container and onto Jimmie's pants, but he had beat it out and rolled on the ground so quickly that they hadn't known he was hurt until later that night when he started limping badly. They cut his pant leg off, and the memory of the boy's ugly bleeding leg was still vivid. He was amazed that it had gotten better, just as they had all been amazed that Watts and the rest of the neighborhoods had gotten better, for a while.

Gangbanging had died out for a while, too, and Jack Brown had joined the Muslims and, subsequently, become Jack Bilal. He hadn't seen Jimmie Black more than once or twice in almost twenty years.

"You're Jimmie Black's son," Mr. Bilal said with the kind of emotion usually associated with long lost relatives.

It caught Jimmie almost totally off guard. He had been prepared to fade into the crowd of faces as he had learned to do for everybody in grown up authority.

"How's your Daddy?"

"Oh, he's doing fine," said Jimmie, though he hadn't seen his daddy in over four years, nor had he planned to get into a conversation with a teacher.

"Next time you see him, tell him you ran into the man who taught him his walk when he lived in Slauson Village."

"You grew up with him, huh?"

"Yeh, your daddy was a part of the riots to get black control of the black community in 1965. He's always been a community hero."

Everybody in the booths was turned, and most of the activity had ceased.

"That was B.C., huh, Mr. Bilal? Before the Crips even started," offered Lamont Branford.

"It was the Slausons, then," continued Mr. Bilal.

"And, the Businessmen," Lamont almost shouted while trying to work his way to the front of the crowd in the narrow aisle through tennis shoed teenagers.

"My Ol' Man was a Bidnessman, and he's got his own business, now. When I'm old enough, he's going to give it to me. Tell 'em, Mr. Bilal, Crippin' is dead. It's about money, now, not blue rags," said Lamont.

"It's not about selling that water or gambling either Lamont. If you'll deal, you'll steal, and get ill, too, Lamont. You better stop selling that death. What about your basketball game? You keep sucking that death down in your chest, and you're gonna lose your hops and never play for the 'Shaw." Mr. Bilal would slap your face with the truth. He turned back toward Jimmie.

"Yeh, son, your father was one of the youngest black freedom fighters in this city. We caused a lot of changes that week in August, 1965, and our message swept this country, the world. The black man would no longer accept oppression. Get your feet off our necks. Call off your police dogs or we'll meet you in the streets.

"A lot of people had to die to get the message across, but it brought everybody in the neighborhoods together. If you ran in a preacher's house hiding from the cops that week, that preacher would hide you. Gangbangers and gangsters all came together to fight the common enemy. Afterwards gangbanging kind of died. You had to be associated with some political organization -- the US organization, Panthers, Muslims, CORE, NAACP, B.S.U. or something. We all had the same sign, then, the closed fist -- like this!"

Bilal then thrust his first skyward proudly in the Black Power salute, beckoned to Weldon and Jimmie with his other hand, and turned walking thru the door toward Mann.

Jimmie found himself walking fast down Florence toward school, unconsciously, never having intended to attend school that day.

"I need you, Li'l Jimmie," said Mr. Bilal as they walked. "I've got to bring the Rollin' 60's and the Eight Tray Gangsters back together again, and I need you to help me."

"I don't think that can happen, Cuzz... c-cause," stuttered Jimmie, catching himself talking to the teacher like he was cool.

Bilal didn't react noticeably, but Jimmie saw in the way he kept walking and smiling that he didn't consider himself the police like the other teachers did. Jimmie continued, seriously...

"There's been over a hundred murders in that gang war, and I just can't see some people quittin'."

"You claiming Rollin' 60?"

"Nah."

"Eight Tray?"

"Naw."

"Come on. Don't diss me, Jimmie. I know you're Crippin'. You think I'm dumb?"

"Oh, no, but I'm O.G. Hoover, and I claim everything in Watts cause my birthright. I'm down with the 60's and most Trays, but I just consider myself O.G. Crip. Straight like that."

"You down for putting an end to the gang wars?" asked Mr. Bilal, abruptly.

Jimmie almost replied without thinking, but he considered it, then said, "Yeh. I'd like to see Crips stop fightin' Crips, but I don't wanna see Crippin' end. Why?"

"I just wanted to know where your head was, Jim. That's the right answer. Now, we've got to get you back in school," said Mr. Bilal, leading them thru the south door of Horace Mann and into the head counselor's office.

It was the beginning of a new life for Jimmie Black, Jr.

Chapter 17
Jimmie Jr.'s Favorite Teacher

It surprised Jimmie that Mr. Bilal didn't expect him to have straight F U U's on his report card.

"You didn't even pass homeroom. But, now you're registered to me. You probably won't go to grad nite or graduation, Jimmie. You've got to start coming to school daily. So, meet me at the OX every morning at 7:30. If I'm late or miss you, eat and meet me in Room 203 at the top of the stairs on the right in the main building before the 10 minute bell rings. If you have trouble, tell everybody you're in Mr. Bilal's homeroom, they'll back up."

"There's some pretty serious stuff goin' down, Mr. Bilal, and I think I oughta tell you that I get high, and I might get into a coupla fights."

"Well, you gonna stop because there are narcs on campus, and you're no good to me in jail. This is business. I'm not looking for no excuses for not taking care of business. This is F.O.I. (Fruit of Islam)."

Jimmie didn't know what it meant, but he knew it was serious business, and something about Mr. Bilal reminded him of his daddy, so he followed him up the stairs.

Weldon followed them, awed that Jimmie had cut into the teacher that everybody was trying to cut into at Mann -- in public speaking, his play, get a poem in his anthology, or a place in his public speaking choir. It had taken Weldon years to work his way to the top spot in Mr. Bilal's South Central L.A. Speech Choir, so he could perform for graduation, and Jimmie Black had walked up on him and gotten carte blanche in one day. It was Jimmie's style. Mr. Bilal was right. Jimmie was definitely a S. Central L.A. thoroughbred. His whole demeanor said, "Win." How could his pops try to keep him from running with somebody like Jimmie?

'School was so smooth,' thought Jimmie. 'Now, people treated him good, like he was somebody. Mr. Bilal took him to the attendance office and introduced him to Mrs. Garvey, the lady who was running it. (As if Jimmie and everybody that ever darkened that attendance office door had not heard, "The Blatherer.")

'But it was so different, now. The lady who had been one Big Mouth to him before, was joking with him about missing so much school and giving him lunch tickets. She reminded him of somebody. He couldn't quite remember who. Somebody real nice in his past.'

Then something happened that shook Jimmie up. The white vice-principal stopped him in the hall, shook his hand, and introduced himself. He didn't even watch as Jimmie ran up the stairs two at a time checking for the graffiti he had left the last time he had been at Mann. Usually, he would ask a couple of the 60's who had crossed out his name and go looking for them. He would probably catch them by nutrition and be back out on the streets by 1:00 P.M. or so. Maybe eat one or two meals before he left. But, this time Jimmie turned right, into Mr. Bilal's room at the top of the stairs.

It startled him. It didn't look like a classroom, really. It had a wide aisle in the middle, and a cameraman was perched on one side focusing a TV camera. He and Mr. Bilal were talking about a show that they were evidently going to do in the room, today. Jimmie slipped quietly into the first seat next to the door as he came in. Soon, the room was filled with kids practicing. A girl came and signed Jimmie into homeroom 203 and smiled at him, and she wasn't the kind of girl that smiled at Crips, either.

It stimulated him, sexually. His mind drifted into scheming, but it was soon caught up in the activity of the room. Mr. Bilal was the center of everything, barking directions, coaching and cajoling the people who were obviously going to perform. Weldon and the Bastille brothers were always nearby running errands, helping the cameraman, asking questions, and constantly practicing on this poetry.

It was like rap, but there wasn't any music. There was music in the room, though, because Cody, Watts Slim, and Coldman were throwing poplock moves to a tape of "Perfect Beat".

It was a regular homeroom class in other respects because they were passing him these information cards to be filled out -- white ones and yellow ones and red ones all wanting you to remember the same lies. "Telephone Number": 'Cut off. No, can't write that. What was it she said to say? Out of order, yeah, out of order.'

Jimmie did his best to fill out the white card then gave still smiling Sheila the red and yellow ones to duplicate for him. She seemed more than happy to do it.

All of a sudden everybody's conversation seemed to change, dropped to a whisper and focused on one girl who had come in the room. Jimmie couldn't understand for the life of him why. She wasn't cute. She was fat. She wasn't even talking loud, but when the cameraman counted:

"Three, Two, One," and pointed, this girl gave the best speech Jimmie had ever heard. She talked about how black people had been slaves, but slave days were over, and she talked about a lot of famous black people who had fought and died so that slave stuff could come to an end. Somehow, Jimmie remembered the name Harriet Tubman, but most of the other names he forgot. Of course, she said Martin Luther King had died for it.

Her hands moved like an actress, and her voice was big like a man's but sweet like a woman's. She recited a poem called, "Hey, Black Child" at the end, and the words echoed in his head: "Do you know you can be what you wanna be if you try to be what you can be..."

Was she looking at him? She looked at him like she meant him most of all, but he didn't feel uncomfortable.

"Do you know you can be what you want to be if you try to be what you can be?"

He had never wanted to be anything but O.G. Crip (respected on the streets), but when he looked at the camera, and it was pointing at him, then he looked at the color TV and saw himself throw up a Playboy Crip sign, he knew he wanted this. So, he decided to fall in line with Weldon and the rest of the kids in Homeroom 203.

His foster parent, Mrs. Fletcher, was only slightly aware that he had started attending school regularly. She and her husband were separated, for the most part, but they did not want to lose the money that the county paid for keeping Jimmie, so Mr. Fletcher came over whenever the man from the county came to visit, but, otherwise, they had a shouting screaming relationship, now.

They both seemed to want a baby but never at the same time. Sometimes, they had screamed names at each other that Jimmie didn't really understand, but he knew they were mad at each other for not being able to have a baby.

Mrs. Fletcher no longer even tried to pretend she wanted to be his mother. She did what she could for him, but he had the responsibility of raising himself because she had her own problems. Until recently, Jimmie had only slept there nightly and occasionally eaten a weekend meal while looking at television with her.

She had SELECT cable and looked at TV all the time. One night he had watched the dirty movie with her. They never talked to each other much, anyway. But, while that movie was on, neither of them said a word. It was strange. He had seen a lot of movies like that but never with an adult, especially a lady.

He couldn't tell from the look on her face what was going through her mind as the couples were doing everything that anybody had ever thought about doing to each other. He was sitting next to her on the sofa, and he started to feel himself losing control of his body, so he started to move away, when her hand reached over and firmly pushed his leg down. Her eyes still on the TV, she said,

"You don't have to leave. You've got to find out about this sooner or later."

The movie seemed to last all night, and when he woke, the TV and lights were cut off, and Mrs. Fletcher had put a cover over him. He went to the bathroom and came back, but could not sleep -- the movie scenes still lingering in his mind. He masturbated forgetting he was on the couch. He dozed hoping Mrs. Fletcher would not find any traces.

She must not have because she never mentioned it, but he never watched dirty movies with her again.

Chapter 18
Jimmie Jr. Turns Around

School had become Jimmie's greatest delight. He looked forward to every morning because he wanted to be one of the first to get up on Western Avenue to the Golden Ox and walk Mr. Bilal to Horace Mann. He had even started doing his homework, hastily and messily, but he was reading heavily. Mr Bilal had started off "dropping books on his head". First his book, the <u>O.G. Poetry Book</u> about the Rollin' 60's and the Eight Trays. It was rhymes written by students from Mann, some of whom he even knew. It was about gangbanging and the pictures were drawn by D-Dog and Dmitri, the two best gang artists on the streets.

It fascinated Jimmie. He had always associated feeling good with getting high, eating, or sex, but not books. How could you explain this feeling? It was good to know books could make you feel like this. Then, Mr. Bilal gave him poetry: "Li'l Brown Baby," "Same in Blues". He laughed at it and loved it. He even practiced saying it. He was a long way from Jewel Robinson, the girl who had first hypnotized him with her speech, and, in fact, most of the Speech Choir members were much better than he was, but he was getting better all the time, and he was reading every black poem that he could get his hands on.

"Gangs Are Us," Mr. Bilal wrote on the board. "They've always been us, our brothers, our sisters, cousins, uncles, neighbors. What are we going to do, cut off our legs because they have a sore on them? To please who? The police?"

Jimmie had never heard anybody in authority talk positively about Crippin', but Mr. Bilal had talked like nobody in authority ever since he first met him. It had been so different since they had first met on Florence at the Golden Ox that morning. It made him feel dignified and proud to be what he was.

"We have always lived in or near jungles, even in Africa, and it is dangerous to walk in jungles at night. There are a lot of snakes, awaiting. They fight each other and they feed on the helpless and small. That metaphor applies to your everyday life. Be careful on these streets at nights. Know your enemy. Respect him. It will make him respect you."

Bilal felt good talking to the gapemouthed youngsters. He wasn't as good as he knew he had to be, yet, but he could almost talk straight to a lot of the youngsters. And, when he could, he planned to drop atom bombs on their brains.

"See, when you allow yourself to be defined by letting the police label you a 'gang member', you open yourself wide open for a bust. You're almost totally at another man's mercy.

"It's time you admitted to being organized, so you can begin to organize better. You are an organization if you are a Crip. You are organized for revolution in the neighborhood, and that's a tough spot to stand on. If you are always wrong, you won't last long.

"You gotta do some good, too, especially in your family. I don't care if you're Rollin' 60 or Eight Tray Gangster. If your momma don't even like you, you gonna do time. You better get some money, fast, or you going to jail.

"Stop thinking like a snake. I used to think I was a snake, too. Low down and dirty. Slimy at times. I'm glad I got out of it."

It seemed to Jimmie that Mr, Bilal talked in riddles that kind of figured themselves out. He always left you thinking and kept you working.

First, he had been ashamed when people would ask him about running errands for Mr. Bilal, but it made him feel so good to have some responsibility for a change. It was like he had been nagged all his life, but he never had felt it was important that he did something correctly: "take out the trash; vacuum clean; etc."

Dirt had not bothered him that much. What had bothered him all his life was fools. Jimmie had always felt that he was going to have to kill a fool or two before he got much older, but that, now, seemed so remote. Even the fools (most of them, anyway) had fallen in line. They no longer even pestered him. They just let him walk by like he was white or invisible or something. In fact, even the white people smiled at him.

It was strange for awhile, then it struck him one day when he was walking fast up Florence toward Western, coming home late from school after practice for the 8th grade pinning ceremony, when he spied Termite coming out of the alley behind Greene's Stationery store.

"What it is? What it was, what that "C" like, Cuzz?" Termite was effusive. It meant he was on the hustle or the beg. It didn't matter to him.

"The Make, Cuzz. I'm on the make for some gappers to fill up some of these gaps in my pocket. I'll even take some geeters just to get started," laughed Termite, eyeing the ladies and their pocketbooks at the bus stop (too many men waiting, too).

"Let's go steal a tape and turn it, Slick Jimmie, you know we good crime partners, Cuzz."

Jimmie stopped and backed all the way up in the service station off the sidewalk.

"I ain't Crippin', Mite." the words came out overly loud and his jaw was set more firmly than he had meant for it to be. The people at the bus stop turned as if they expected a fight.

"What you lookin' at?" said Termite turning on an S.A. who was waiting for the bus half turned in the direction of their loud conversation.

"You two going to fight or what?" said the S.A. taking a cholo stand, one shoe pointed perpendicularly at Termite and planted midway against his other shoe.

"Get some bizness, homeboy, and stay out of mine," taunted Termite as he and Jimmie proceeded east across Western Avenue.

"Yeh, you know, Jimmie?" he said under his breath. "You don't even look like you Crippin', anymore."

Jimmie had gotten his act together too late to graduate from Horace Mann, but he was as happy about graduation as anybody. His grades were above "C" in every class, and that made him eligible for activities, and there were activities daily. The class picnic, the awards assembly, the dances, the talent shows, the speech contests. It just went on and on, and Mr. Bilal had a hand in everything that happened on the stage which meant Jimmie was right there, too. Everybody started calling him his daddy.

It made Jimmie smile, but the real reason he had opened himself up so much to Mr. Bilal was that he talked about Big Jimmie and knew him.

Jimmy knew that if anybody could find his daddy, it was Mr. Bilal.

It was strange. Everybody knew Jimmie Black Sr., but nobody had seen him in four years since he had been released from jail, it seemed.

When Jimmie Jr. would hop off the bus on Florence and Vermont and shake down the brothers at the Winchell's Donut Shop about his daddy, they would tell long adventures (often mixed with laughter) about the old days, but nobody had seen him.

They would just say check the mosque over on Central or Crenshaw. But, Jimmie was scared to go to the mosque.

"Yeh, yo' daddy's the one who killed all them people and got away with it. I sure ain't seen him, but if I do I'll sure tell him you're lookin' for him."

Jimmie took the compliments and backhanded praise (challenges) with the same demeanor. He'd known these men all of his life, but never really understood why they stood in front of liquor stores and hung out in donut shops. At first, he had thought it was sex because they harassed most females, but as Jimmie, himself, began to mature, he saw that among "men" they were decidedly mediocre. Lady Tee sometimes would turn a trick with one of them and give him the money. They lied to each other constantly. "Pulled each others' morals down," his daddy had said.

Li'l Jimmie flashed his bus pass and turned so sharply on his Adidas powering his way toward the back of the bus that everybody took notice. By the time he pushed his way to the back he knew something was wrong.

Eight Trays were holding down the front of the bus, and 60's were talking much head in the back. All the hip people were getting off on Budlong because it was definitely "on".

The bus driver was frozen by the sight of two Trays (J-Dog and Zacky) who were strapped down with pieces and obviously going to shoot him if he made a false move. A few weeks ago this would have been the kind of situation that made Jimmie's blood foam and fret with anticipation. He went straight to Tique in the back of the bus -- Uzi on his lap.

"What up?"

"Your homeboy killed two 60's on Western Ave. last night, so we been killin' Trays all day, J-Rock," Tique said cooly.

The bus crossed Vermont, barely got into second gear before easing to the Budlong Avenue stop. Jimmie, standing in the crowded aisle, turned slightly to see Weldon making his way toward him through the crowd that was pushing toward the rear exit.

All of a sudden from the front of the just cleared aisle of the bus Mobster jumped out of his seat and screamed,"Somebody gotta die!"

The carbine spit four rounds down the aisle. Jimmie anticipated the first one and raced it, lunging for Weldon. He felt the impact of the bullet as he pushed Weldon to the floor of the bus. The other bullets zinged over their squirming bodies as Jimmie pulled Weldon behind a seat.

When the carbine paused, Mobster leaped to cover just as Tique stood up in the back of the bus and turned the Uzi loose. It tore out all the windows in the front, but when it began to ricochet off the steel handles of the seats, he eased up on the trigger.

The bus driver had managed to reopen the front door and run down Budlong between barrages of the machine gun.

The seconds were pregnant with decision making. Jimmie knew he and Weldon had to sit tight and, if anything, try to talk their way out of it. There was so much blood coming out of Weldon onto Jimmie's shirt that he wasn't sure the bullet hadn't somehow pierced his own body, but there was no burning, so he was all right. For sure, there was no getting around the metal partition and out the back door.

All of a sudden the sirens pierced the air from East and West on Florence. The helicopters could be heard approaching. Mobster and the Trays slipped out of the front of the bus and the 60's started running out of the back.

The first squad car approached the bus warily, its officers fanning out on both sides of Florence. Jimmie could hear the police screaming warnings and threats as they approached the bus from the rear. The Trays and 60's were long gone, but Jimmie knew better than to stand up quickly. As hyped up and maddened as the police sounded, they would shoot first and clean it up later. Instead he screamed.

"I'm shot!"

A lady cop got to them first. She asked if he could stand. He said he could, but he didn't think Weldon (now passed out under him) could. The paramedics came and carried Weldon's limp body to the ambulance. Jimmie was determined not to leave him, and they weren't sure he was unscathed himself, so he climbed in behind the procession of paramedics.

The crowd was beginning to form, now, assured, again, of their safety. The original bus riders began to tell their grisly detailed stories to the police. Those who had in some way interacted, overseen, or overheard the incident began to discuss it with eye witness accuracy. They hoped the T.V. cameras would come. It had happened, however, at a very inopportune time for T.V. news, late afternoon.

The police officer that seemed to be in charge had said, "It was a shootout between the 60's and Trays. Looks like two 60's got wounded. One of them may possibly die."

As the ambulance began to speed east on Florence, Jimmie could see the first cars begin to slowly rush their ways past the demolished bus, through the glass and blood. Twenty minutes later, traffic had resumed its brisk pace on Florence, and, to the rest of the world, the incident had never even occurred.

Chapter 19

Revenge

After they took Jimmie to Martin Luther King Hospital and found out he was all right, Nurse Shelley, who was now nursing supervisor, looked over the policeman's shoulder who was filling out his report.

"Is that boy's name Jimmie Black?" she said, startled.

"Yeh, he was in a gang shootout," said the black officer, turning toward her. "You know him?"

Nurse Shelley scanned the faces of the patients until she saw Jimmie standing uneasily by the emergency room door. He was so much taller and more handsome. He was thin but muscular. His hair, which she had always admired, was cut in the jheri curl style without the grease.

When their eyes met briefly, she saw no recognition in his. It stabbed at her. Though she had suffered through two cosmetic surgeries (tummy tuck and face lift), she knew that her good looking days were long gone. The pride she had once had in her sexy figure and fetching smile had been transferred to pride in her accomplishments on the job and her possessions. She could afford to buy good looks, now, if she needed them for special occasions. The white, neatly tailored, nurse's outfit required much too much cloth to cover her ample proportions, and since she had also been talked into a hysterectomy by an old O.B.-GYN boyfriend, her appetite was greater for food than sex.

Yet, there was a passion building up inside her for him. This youngster whose daily existence, undoubtedly, was shrouded with ignorance and juxtaposed to all she had come to worship in society had provoked a strange longing in her breasts to embrace him, comfort him, love him, openly...

"No, no. I don't know him, but I do know you've got to hurry up and get him out of here. There's too much commotion in this emergency room, and the sooner y'all, leave, the better," said Nurse Shelley, asserting her authority. Jimmie gave them the information they needed to contact Weldon's parents. When the officer asked about his own parents, he said that he didn't have any, so the policeman took him to 77th Street Precinct to be questioned.

Jimmie didn't want to leave Weldon, so he had put up a fuss, and they had handcuffed him and taken him to the patrol car.

At the police station, Jimmie maintained that he and Weldon were just riding the bus when the shooting broke out. And, they knew nothing about a gang war.

The police could neither confirm nor disprove what he said, but since he didn't have a responsible adult to be released to, he had to sit tight. There were so many gang murders happening that they wanted to hold on to any suspects in case something else happened.

By the time Mr. Bilal came towards the desk in the squad room where Jimmie was being questioned, the thought had already begun to take shape in the boy's mind. There was a weird calmness that came with it, as if there was no longer a need for apprehension about it. He knew, now, that he was going to do a murder, and he knew who he was going to kill. It would probably take him weeks, maybe months, but Mobster was going to die if he had to follow him into jail.

Mr. Bilal had all the details about the shootings in the last 24 hours. Lamont, Ken Bone, and Hollister had started selling the new drug, Crack (cocaine) instead of coming to school. They had gone big time, however, because they had direct connections with a South American through the 60's, so they were setting up all the Wanna Be's with drugs. They were taking over corners for drive thru drug sales and swooping down heavy with the artillery whenever there was a conflict.

They were spreading out so fast and dealing so much crack that rumors were out that all three of them had become millionaires in just a few months. Lamont was for sure.

Termite (who was now claiming Eight Tray and supplying most of the Wanna Be Trays out of his black on black Cadillac coupe de ville) had gotten jealous, so he road down on them partying in the liquor store parking lot on 69th and Western. They hadn't known Termite was a Tray when they set their Olde English bottles down and stepped into the alley to toke some of Termite's drugs.

Termite had come out the pocket on them with a .357 magnum, killing Hollister and Ken Bone instantly, the pipes still in their hands as the gigantic rounds forced their heads against the back wall of the Chinese food restaurant before penetrating deeply into their brains. Lamont had managed to get away, though wounded.

Tique (who had just gotten out of California Youth Authority) and the shooters from the 60's had retaliated quickly. Not having a car big enough to carry all of them, they had simply jumped on the Western Avenue bus, dismounted on Manchester, shot up St. Andrews Park, and walked down Manchester through the Eight Tray 'hood killing Trays.

They took the Manchester bus down to Broadway and the Broadway to Florence where they were spotted. The Trays had caught up with them at Florence and Hoover. Mobster had led the large group of heavily armed Trays onto the bus, and they had staked out the front just before Jimmie and subsequently Weldon had gotten on at Vermont.

"Jimmie," Mr. Bilal said, pulling up in front of Jimmie's house, "you better be super cool cause the word is out that you were banging with the 60's when it happened, and the Trays are saying you're a mark. You sure you don't wanna stay with me for a while or somewhere else? You know this is the Eight Tray 'hood."

"Nah, Mr. Bilal, everything's cool. Just let me know about Weldon. If anything happens, let me know. I'll be hanging around home for a while. And, don't worry. None of the Trays know where I stay except Termite, and I know he wouldn't tell."

When Mr. Bilal drove off, Jimmie knocked on the door, but Mrs. Fletcher was not at home, so he sat on the steps and waited. Mrs. Fletcher came home a little later. She opened the door with the perfunctory greeting, caught up completely in her own problems.

Chapter 20
ALLAHŪ AKBAR!

The next morning Jimmie was sitting on his porch. It depressed him to think about the future. He knew he was probably going to jail for a while, but he had to kill Mobster.

All the stuff he had ever said in his life didn't mean anything if he didn't. Mobster had shot and probably killed his homeboy, Weldon, and Weldon didn't even bang.

A cream colored Rolls Royce with a tan top pulled up in front of the house directly across the street. If stopped and there seemed to be at least four well dressed men in it.

The passenger door on the street side opened and Ray Ray barged out. He was dressed expensively, but Jimmie had been seeing him all his life, and his look and manner were unmistakable.

Ray Ray was up the steps and on the porch before Jimmie realized the scenario included him this time. He had seen Ray Ray, often, asserting himself on the streets. Termite and Jimmie had practiced his walk, half jesting, but never had he spoken to him except for once or twice when he had nodded acknowledging Jimmie's waves.

Jimmie knew that Ray Ray knew his daddy well, and they had been original members of the Crips, but some people said the police told Ray Ray what to do now.

"Whassup, Cuzz... Li'l Jimmie?" Ray Ray stood over Jimmie who was still seated on the steps. Jimmie realized that if he stood, he would be taller than this "man", not a supernatural being. He sat on the .38 that he had taken from Mrs. Fletcher's hiding place in her room, and he felt secure that he could meet even Ray Ray's challenge.

Then three gangsters got out of the Rolls Royce and sat on the porch. They were obviously strapped down with pieces at least as big as the .38.

"What that 107 O.G. Crip "C" like?" said Jimmie grabbing Ray Ray's extended hand and hugging him.

"I hear you got trouble from the Trays and the 60's, Cuzz. You know, I ain't surprised. I been watching you, Jimmie. I been asking around about you. I known you a long time -- since you were born. When I see your momma, she tells me what's happening with you. You got in with some tough youngsters..."

"I ain't no Sixty," Jimmie said, sitting back down on the loaded .38 that had been exposed when he stood up to embrace.

"I know it, but that Hollister and them 60's were some tough li'l gangsters. You were backing their play on the streets, Jimmie, and that boy, Mobster, thinks you were fightin' <u>with</u> them on that bus."

"Well, I say it ain't got to be like he say."

Jimmie began to blurt out the details of what happened on the bus. Mrs. Fletcher came to the screen door, sheepishly. Ray Ray froze her with a wry smile.

"Hi you doin', Sherry? I talk to you, baby, a little later on." She went away so fast; it was as if she had never appeared.

"Don't worry about it, Cuzz. I'm going to take care of it for you. I can cool out Mobster cause he works for me," bragged Ray Ray shaking his head encouragingly at the gangsters sitting around the porch.

"Yeh, and the 60's doing business with you, Cuzz, so we can clear up any misunderstandings with them," chimed in Murder Mouse whom Jimmie hardly recognized in a suit.

"I want chu to work for me, Jimmie. See most Crips are too nomadic. They jump from one thing to another, no discipline, Cuzz. You can't count on 'em to do business. I know you got what it takes to make a lot of money, and plus you a true Crip. I want chu with <u>me</u>." Ray Ray grinned.

"Doin' what? Dealin'? Slangin'?" Jimmie spat in disgust. He and Weldon had vowed to never sell crack or use it, and he wasn't about to let anybody turn him out on a street corner selling drugs.

"Naw, you'll be the slangers' boss. That's what I want you to do. Just go with me when I have to spread around a big piece, and keep your eyes open and your mouth shut.

"You can stay right here with Sherry Fletcher and park a BMW in the driveway."

Jimmie knew what Ray Ray was saying was true because it was happening all around him -- fifteen year olds driving BMW's and Benz's paying cash for them. It would have sounded great a few weeks ago, but recently, that life of crime did not seem so sublime. Doing time hadn't seemed an eventuality, recently, either. But, that was before yesterday. Now, it didn't matter, again. He was going to kill Mobster and working for Ray Ray was the perfect cover.

He didn't know if he seemed happy enough when he accepted Ray Ray's offer. Ray Ray seemed to be happy, but Mouse and the other gangsters kind of sneered at him like, "You don't even know what you gettin' into."

Ray Ray pushed past the crowd on the porch and into the house. Mrs. Fletcher tried to hug him, but he played her off. They talked for a moment, and Ray Ray went in his pocket and gave her a package. She was just too thankful as he and his entourage made their way out of the neat little two story stucco and back toward the Rolls.

"We'll pick you up tomorrow, Li'l Jimmie. Wear a suit, If you got a hat, wear it, Cuzz."

"Ray Ray," Jimmie called after them, "It's J-Rock, okay?"

That night Mr. Bilal called and said Weldon was still in a coma. Jimmie told him that he wouldn't be coming to school for a while.

"Maybe it's best, Jim. I'm going to try to talk to as many kids as possible at school and cool this thing out, but it is probably better for you to stay at home for a few days."

Jimmie was glad he didn't have to lie to Mr. Bilal because he knew he couldn't tell him that he was quitting school. It would have meant a big lecture, and, in fact, Mr. Bilal might even try to talk him out of it.

"You be careful, yourself," said Jimmie, trying to be assertive, but coming off too slick, secretive.

That night Termite was killed at the street racers' and gangbangers' hangout on Florence and Main. Everybody was scared to talk about it at Mann the next day. Termite, at one time, had attended Mann, briefly. He was well known as a Pac Man junkie and Wanna Be Crip on Western Avenue. It wasn't apparent, until then, that people were going to be continually dying.

Mr. Bilal was a veritable explosion of energy. He had a hastily scheduled assembly at 10:00 A.M., and he was operating the dean's office out of the auditorium, so he would be sure to get all the gangsters before the day was over and counsel them in small groups. The poets and musicians had done three proper performances by the time the assembly formally began.

When Mr. Bilal took the microphone to M.C. the assembly, the auditorium was filled with a deafening roar of belligerence. The lights had been brought up to silence the myriad of verbal and physical scuffles.

"BE QUIET... SHUT UP! THIS IS MAY 19TH, MALCOLM X'S BIRTHDAY.

"WE'RE GOING TO TALK ABOUT STRUGGLE?" said Bilal above the cacophony of voices.

When they realized in harmony that Tina Marie's "Deja Vu" was wooing them, and Mr. Bilal was talking in that rhythmic staccato, it coaxed them into cohesion. They became Mann. HORSE MANN! And, they exploded with applause for their most effective teacher.

"Introducing one of you. A strong voice and a handsome youth, Mr. Michael Bastille, doing the Langston Hughes classic... 'Notes on Commercial Theater,' for our beloved Weldon Brown." And, the audience broke into applause as Michael recited the poem that Weldon had made one of their favorites.

"You've taken my blues and gone..."

It was as if he put his whole heart into it, and everybody felt the same way (even the Trays in the audience). Weldon lay dying in the hospital, and everyone loved him. Jackie Henry began comforting Quintana who was crying in the front row.

It was a blues assembly. Michael's brother, Ray, did "The Weary Blues" with Tyrece Jackson accompanying on guitar. Jewel Robinson brought the house down with James Weldon Johnson's "Go Down Death." (The actors on the mourning bench were falling all over the stage so, people didn't know whether to laugh or cry.)

Then Mr. Bilal resumed his position at the podium. He had all the lights brought up and began to stare into people's eyes. It was as if he was reading their minds.

"If we must die, let us not die young and drugged and drunk... trying to make meaning out of misery... for false pride, or PCPeed, hated and pitied. Let it not be like dogs trapped in fast feud shootouts. Better to let it be against God's enemies, and, yeh. He has many.

"If we <u>must</u> die, let it be fighting the Klu Klux Klan -- biting, fighting, striking any kind of blow against an enemy of righteous man. Your momma, at least, won't have to die too, like if you get shot in a gangbanging shootout. She, at least, wouldn't have to feel so blue (shamed by a liar born in her moment of lust/frustration).

"If you must die young, why die at the hands of the enemy of the moment, and be another monument to vehement ignorance? You better live and outlive the foolishness of this time when things have made a change for the worse, as a sign, and many a teenager is going to be killed, mistakenly, by this lifetaking cycle of hating.

"First, you are alive and dying, denying and not trying. Living in fear and fading into immoral obscurity. Stooping to smoking instead of studying and quoting <u>wino</u> philosophers. Patterning your lives after television blight -- daylight, trite, popeyed, cartoon heroes and young and restless zeroes whose consciences are dying as much as your own, and who teach you fighting (as the first solution) and dying drenched with weeping and wishes for one drop of wisdom before you fall into the hole. Timing enough to say, yes, instead of, no. Wisdom to know when to walk fast instead of slow. When to be and what to be to walk free in <u>your own</u> community.

"Don't choose the snakefilled path and regret every day until death at last lifts the painful load of ignorance exploded as a mercy to you and our community... enslaved by youth that curse truth.

"It is becoming fashionable for you to waste your youth in prolonged lazy stupidity, retarded morality, 40 oz. fantasies, cracked dreams, and stunted intellectual growth... which, eventually, take it from me, promotes a desire for death.

"But, if you're thinking about dying young and for nothing, why not live a while longer until you get a little stronger struggling to hold on -- Scratching and biting and fighting -- to carry on the responsibility for breeding and breathing more life into your own children, someday, when you survive to see... TO LIVE! ... YOUR OWN BEAUTIFUL SELVES RECREATED."

Then Jewel Robinson came out and recited "Hey, Black Child," and everybody left that auditorium feeling ten feet tall. Everybody just backed way off even talking about killing. It was as if every individual in that auditorium had been touched by a spirit, and the world was going to have a tough time getting it out of them even after they left and went back to class.

That night there were no murders, and as Jack Bilal came into the burger stand the next morning he felt somewhat relieved. He saw Lamont sitting at a table in the corner, walked over and sat.

"Lamont, you all right? You still hurt?"

"Yeh, well, I don't have any bullets in me anymore, but I'm sore. I'm coming back to school, Mr. Bilal. I'm gonna try to get my hops back and play some basketball. I think I can still graduate."

"What about the fast life, Lamont? I heard you had an awful lot of money last week."

"I ain't got nothin', Mr. Bilal. I got ripped off for everything while I was in the hospital. I can't even help my daddy pay for my hospital bills. I thought about trying to recover some of it, but my daddy said to let it go. I'm just gonna put it behind me and thank God I'm alive."

"You mean you and the 60's aren't down for trying to kill some Trays for what they did to Hollister and Ken Bone?" said Bilal, surprised.

"I can't do nothin' about it and don't even wanna anymore. So many people have died that all of the young gangsters are probably gonna back up... at least, for a while, except for maybe Jimmie Black," said Lamont.

"What's happening with Jimmie!"

"I saw him last night, and he's packing a .357 magnum and dressing gangster. He's running with the biggest dope dealers, and I <u>know</u> J-Rock. First chance he gets, he's going to kill Mobster for what he did to Weldon."

Suddenly, it struck Jack Bilal. It had been there in

his tone Sunday night. Jimmie had gotten turned out for the gangster life again. This time it would take something awfully strong to turn him around.

Mrs. Fletcher stood in her living room window peeking out from behind the curtain, apprehensively, at the two men who waited for Jimmie on her front porch. One was that nosy teacher and the other (who Mr. Bilal introduced as his brother) looked like a cop.

As Jimmie stepped out of the limo, he saw them. There was a surge of emotion when he saw his daddy. If he had been younger, he would have run up and hugged him. The emotions were almost uncontrollable... then, he realized that somebody must have told Mr. Bilal what he was doing. It sobered him.

"As Salaamu Alaikum," said Yusuf, measuring his son, now, almost as tall as himself. Jimmie did not reply.

"What, you don't know me, huh?" said Yusuf, smiling and moving smoothly down the steps toward Jimmie, his hand anticipating his son's.

"How could I forget your hook head?" replied Jimmie smiling slightly and extending his own hand. "You finally decided to look me up, huh? I've been looking for you for 3 years. What up? Why you come see me now?"

Yusuf, sensing his son's righteous indignation, answered with his own question.

"Why didn't you look at the mosque? You know I married again, Jimmie, and I've got two little girls, your sisters, Jamillah and Aminah. My wife, Ihsan, and your sisters really want to meet you."

"Why you just show up, now?" said Jimmie feeling a little unnerved knowing that he had purposely not looked for his daddy at the mosque, and remembering the social workers' oft repeated admonition's about his daddy.

"I came because Jack Bilal came and told me he knew you and that you were going to do a murder."

"You did it. You killed people who needed killing. Even you did it, Mr. Bilal, in the army. Now, you gonna tell me that it's wrong for me cause I'm too young, huh?"

"I never killed anybody in the army, Jimmie. That's probably why I'm alive today. The people that did the most killing in the war are the ones that got killed or who are crazy, today," Mr. Bilal spoke defensively, but in utter sincerity.

"It's overglorified, Jimmie. There's nothing great that's going to happen to you after you kill somebody. It'll make you think you're doomed to the same fate. Decent people will treat you like a freak, if they know. I'll never do it again, Son, and I hope you never have to." There was no doubt in Yusuf's mind that his son, standing before him, body taut with emotion, but not trembling, face flinching with anger, had suffered enough to surpass any act of hatred that even he, himself, had been guilty of.

"You just don't know me. A lot of things have changed since I last saw you. I don't wanna scratch out a living while rich people run the world. I wanna be somebody. I wanna own a lot of things," Jimmie said defiantly.

"By hanging with Ray Ray? By setting up drug sales and strongarming people? Listen to me, Jimmie. It doesn't work out. I KNOW!" screamed his father.

The two men bombarded Jimmie with good reasons for not living the criminal life, but they were stifled when he told them about the empire that Ray Ray had shown him in the last couple of days. Houses, cars, jewelry, cameras, even video cameras, and TV's. It was simply amazing that one person could have so much stuff. Motels and a limousine business made Ray Ray as successful in business as legitimate black businessmen.

It was a challenge to his daddy. Yusuf Bilal had changed his life when he changed his name. He had been unable to talk Carole into changing with him, so he had left her and moved near Masjid Felix Bilal on Central Avenue. He had pursued his education at Cal. State, L.A. as well as at the masjid, and his spirit and dedication had soon brought him his greatest blessing, Ihsan. She was 21, eight years younger than him, when they met, and though he thought her the purest beauty he had ever seen, then, their marriage and her ensuing motherhood had only enhanced her incomparable beauty.

Yusuf, now, taught high school at the Muslim school, Sister Clara Muhammad (though his graduation from college was a year away), and the meager but sufficient living that he now made seemed paltry compared to Ray Ray's fortunes.

To further complicate things, Carole had refused (out of spite) to sign the divorce papers, so he had taken a second wife without the knowledge or consent of the courts. There seemed to be no way that he could untangle the legal web that kept him from having his son until he saved a lot more money for a good lawyer.

"Jimmie, I don't care what the courts say. I want to take you home with me. I've been talking to Jack, and he tells me a lot of good things about you. Let me look out for you. I can't promise you there won't be problems. But, I love you, Son, and I'm not going to sit on the sideline and let you die in these streets."

When Jimmie heard his daddy say he loved him, his eyes filled with tears. He was almost overcome. He caught himself, though.

"I don't have to die. Ray Ray ain't dead. Weldon's dead, and he never killed or hurt anybody in his life!" Jimmie blurted out, struggling unsuccessfully to keep from crying.

"No, Jimmie. Weldon's okay! He's going to be all right. They took the bullet out of his chest, and he's recovering nicely," said Mr. Bilal.

"Weldon's okay? He's all right!" The full meaning of the words was so beautiful. He had just known that Weldon was going to die because of him. He grabbed Mr. Bilal and hugged him.

Then, he turned and looked at his daddy. His defenses down, now, Jimmie hugged him, proudly. It was as though a huge burden had been taken off his back and placed properly on his father's strong shoulders.

"Daddy," he said.

"What?"

"I lied. I wanna be just like you. I always have. I <u>always</u> will."

"Allahu akbar!"*

*God is The Greatest!

SOUTH CENTRAL L.A. DIALECT
(Glossary of Contemporary Slang)

A

"A" (hay) - Hello.

A baller - He or she "got game", has athletic skills (usually basketball), or the person has money.

B

baggin' or baggin' on - Insulting someone.

bangin' - Good in an excellent way; also, gangbangin'.

back the truck up - Say it again.

Benjamins - Hundred dollar bills.

BK - Blood killa. Implies dislike for no other reason than a person belongs to the Blood gang or lives in Blood Nation (a Blood neighborhood).

B.K.A. - Better Known As.

blasted - Very intoxicated.

blazin' - Very nice; or, smoking drugs.

Blood - The Blood Nation, a federation of several street gangs that originated in South Central L.A. in the early 1970's but with roots in Chicago thru BPS (Black P. Stones, L.A. chapter of the Black Stone Rangers, originally). Former arch enemies of the CRIPS before the gang truce.

bomb - Especially good.

bout it - Down; committed; serious about it.

Bro - Brother.

bud - Marijuana.

burnt out - Old; boring.

busta - Scary person.

bust a bitch - Make a U-turn.

C

celly - Cell phone.

chickenhenhead - Girls w/no (very little} hair; or, sometimes generic for girl.

cheese - Money.

chill out! - Calm down! (a command).

CK - Crip killa. Implies dislike for no other reason than a person belongs to the Crip gang or lives in a Crip neighborhood.

clowning - Making jokes about somebody. ("Oh! You got jokes. You trying to clown me, huh?")

Crip - A member of the largest street gang in America. Originally, started by Raymond Washington in the late 1960's, it now has affiliates in most large cities and many small cities in America. The acronym (C.R.I.P.) originally, stood for "Continual (or, Community) Revolution In Progress".

cuzz - Friend; Crip brother.

da - The.   D

datz tight - That's outstanding.

deep - a whole lot, large quantity.

D's - Dayton's (expensive gold tire rims).

dime piece - A good looking boy or girl; rated 10.

dog - Friend or brother; or, to mistreat.

Don't fight it. - Give the person their props (proper respect).

Don't trip. - Calm down.

dope (adj.) - Especially good. "That's dope!"; syn. **bomb**.

Keep it on the **down low, d-low,** or **d.1.** - Keep it private.

Do you wanna catch a fade? also, **take fade** - Fight.

drag - Trite conversation intended to somewhat impress females but also intended to be a macho display.

III

dubb - $20 dollars.

duck - Unattractive person.

Easty - From the East Side of South Central L.A.; low class. E

extra'd out - Not necessary.

faded - High (inebriated). F

fa sho' - Yes.

firmay - Nice. "The bomb".

flossin' - Showing off.

re' real - Really.

for rea' doe - For real.

forty - 40 oz. bottle of malt liquor (The drink of choice for gangs).

fo' sheezee - For sure/positive.

game - Above average basketball skills; or, good "lines" (seductive conversation) for women. G

get back - Talk to me later.

gear - Clothes

ghetto fabulous - Something or someone highly esteemed in the neighborhood.

g-ride - Stolen car.

get your grind on - Slow dance.

grip - A large quantity.

Hey cause! - Hey you! (up-to-date variation on "Hey, Cuzz!") H

hizo - Ho'; promiscuous or a prostitute.

hizzay - House.

ho' box - Pager.

homeboy - Brother, friend.

homie - Friend.

hoochie - Girls who dress sleazy.

IV

hood dz (The Set) - Gang.

hood rat - Someone who has sex indiscriminately in the neighborhood.

hyna - A female.

I be mobbin' - I'm walking like I'm tough.　　　I

I got flows. - I can rap.

ice cream man - Dope man.

In the house or In the hizzay - Here, present.

It's all good. - That's good; or, I don't care.

janky - One who's coldhearted, scandalous; stingy.　　J

jigga - A euphemism for the N-word.

jiggy - Dressed well.

kicking back or kicking it - Relaxing.　　　K

kick rocks - Leave.

knocker - Firearm.

Let's ball out. - Let's go, now.　　　L

Let's bounce - Let's go.

Let go. - Let the situation go, otherwise, let's go.

Let's mob. - A group of people walking.

Lex Lugar - Lexus coupe.

L.I.G. - Let it go.

lock - To fight.

mark - Wimp; or, weak and don't know it.　　　M

mash - To pursue enthusiastically.

molly wop - Butt kicking; to severly beat up.

Move the spot. - Let's go.

Move somethin' - Let's fight.

My bad - Mea culpa; my fault.

Niyyah - The pejorative form of Negro.　　　N

Off the hizzay or Off the hook - Especially good.　O

one time - The police.

V

parlay - Relax.

Pass the rock. - Pass the basketball.

Peep this. - Listen up.

phat - Good; pretty hot and tempting.

pimp - Lady's man, not necessarily a professional.

pimped out - Looks nice.

playahata or hata - One who is jealous.

player - Too good for one person.

po po's - Police

primos - Rock cocaine (crack - the worst drug)

proper - Nice.

props - Proper respect.

put salt in my game - Mess up my plan.

raise up - To stand, not back down; also, leave me alone.   R

rich rollin' - Having money.

riffs - Sheriffs.

ripped - Fully Cripped out in gang attire.

Rollie - Rolex watch.

ryda - Someone who "takes nothing from no one" (demands respect).

S

sauce - Weak in a certain sport.

scanless - Scandalously shameless.

scrap - Fight.

scrella - Money.

set trippin' - Gang's having an altercation.

shake the spot - Leave.

shoot - Play dice.

shorty - A girl.

skinded - Light/dark skinned.

slangin' - Selling drugs.

slippin' - Not paying attention.

Police

- Go away.

- Cool.

Gun.

atted - Tattoo/ tattooed.   T

t my boo. - That's my girlfriend/boyfriend.

at's my baby daddy. - That's my man. (Either we have a child together, or I want to have a child with him).

This is bunk. - This is boring.

3 or Fo's - Ho's, hoodrats.

The tilt - The house.

Toe up from the flo' up. - Old slang that means ugly from head to toe.

24/7 - All the time.

ugly cause - Out of control ugly.   U

We be clubbin' - Partying.   W

We out. - Me and my friends are leaving.

Who that is? Who dat? - Who is that?

Who dis? - Who is this? (telephone greeting)

What hanging? - What's going on?

What in the hizzay - What the Hell?

What's crackin'? also What's crackalackin'? - A Greeting. What's going on?

Why you all up in my Kool Aid and don't even know the flavor? - Why are you meddling in my business and don't know what it's about?

Yay yo - Drugs.   Y

You dipping?/You dipping. - Are you driving?/You are in my business.

Your breath is on hum. - You have bad breath.

You better recognize - Check yourself.